Publication of this book was made possible by a generous gift from
James C. Dunn, Livonia, Michigan

Pre-publication expenses for this book were paid for in part by the
children of Skip and Jean Mehlenbacher
in memory of their parents who loved Isle Royale

Elling Seglem's journals, diaries and photographs were supplied by
his granddaughters
Gloria Covert and Gloria Greenstreet

Acknowledgments:

At Central Michigan University,
Krista Boerman, James Conway, Jon Edwards, Emily Rohde, Matt Salagar, Sarah Sommer,
Crystal Starkey, Heather Trommer, and Sheryl Urias contributed to the transcribing and
editing of manuscripts.

At Isle Royale National Park,
Liz Valencia contributed with archival assistance and photo selection.

Contents:

Seglem's Cabin

Seglem Harbor / Fisherman's Home

8
WEEKS TO A
HEALTHY DOG

8
WEEKS TO A
HEALTHY DOG

An Easy-to-Follow Program for the Life of Your Dog

SHAWN MESSONNIER, D.V.M.
Author of the *Natural Health Bible for Dogs & Cats*

RODALE

Notice

This book is intended as a reference volume only, not as a medical manual. The information given here is designed to help you make informed decisions about your health. It is not intended as a substitute for any treatment that may have been prescribed by your doctor. If you suspect that you have a medical problem, we urge you to seek competent medical help.

Beginning on page 210, you will find safe use guidelines for the herbs recommended in this book that will help you use these remedies safely and wisely.

Mention of specific companies, organizations, or authorities in this book does not imply endorsement by the publisher, nor does mention of specific companies, organizations, or authorities imply that they endorse this book.

Internet addresses and telephone numbers given in this book were accurate at the time it went to press.

ISBN 0-7394-3767-4

Printed in the United States of America

Illustrations by Randy Hamblin
Photograph by Nicki Pardo/Getty

Book design by Joanna Williams

Contents

PART THREE: RESOURCES FOR A HEALTHY DOG

Acknowledgments

First, I would like to thank Dr. Andrew Weil for his inspirational approach to health care. His integrative approach teaches us that we can use the "best of both worlds" by sensibly combining conventional and alternative therapies.

Thanks to my agent, Barbara Collins Rosenberg, for guiding me through the business aspects of writing a book.

Thank you to my editor at Rodale, Ellen Phillips, for your inspiration and passion for this project, and to my project editor, Jennifer Bright Reich, for your enthusiasm and all your hard work.

Thanks to all of my clients, who are open to trying new therapies and who seek healing for your pets. I have shared some of your success stories in *8 Weeks to a Healthy Dog*, and I know they will serve as inspiration for readers everywhere.

I would also like to thank all of the readers of my previous holistic health books and current readers of my weekly pet column, "The Holistic Pet," distributed around the world by Knight Ridder News Service. Thank you for all your questions and support: I know I'm on the right path! Thanks also to the editor of my column, Paula Watson, for giving me a platform to help hundreds of thousands of pets each week.

Thanks to Jennifer Degtjarewsky at www.ivillage.com, who allows me to share my holistic vision with millions of visitors to the Web site each month.

Thank you to Bob Vella, host of *PetTalk America*. Your show is changing the way we care for our pets, and your listeners are always hospitable to me when I'm a guest on the show and help them solve their pet-care problems.

As always, thanks to Dr. Robert Silver, who has answered many holistic questions for me, and whom I continue to think of as a long-distance mentor and friend.

Thanks, too, to Craig Kisciras of Rx Vitamins for Pets, Mike Murphy of MVP Laboratories, and John Kuck of Animal Health Options, all of whom admire my work, promote the cause of using quality supplements for pet wellness, and offer pet owners everywhere the best supplements available to help heal pets.

Finally, love and kisses to my wife, Sandy, and daughter, Erica. Your support is always appreciated, and I cherish the time we share together. (I wish my days and nights were not so hectic!)

Welcome
to Our 8-Week Program

I'm Dr. Shawn Messonnier, and I'd like to welcome you to the 8 Weeks to a Healthy Dog Program. I think you and your dog will enjoy participating in the program, and I can guarantee that your dog will be healthier and happier—and the two of you will be closer than ever—in just eight short weeks from now.

Why did I create the 8 Weeks to a Healthy Dog Program? Because the way owners and their veterinarians are looking at pet health care has begun to change, and it's time for a new road map to pet care. You're holding that map in your hands right now!

Here's what's happening in the field of animal medicine: Over the last few years, the veterinary profession has seen a major paradigm shift. Slowly, the focus is moving away from vaccinating all pets with every vaccine available. Instead, veterinarians are taking a look at each pet's individual needs.

This is a major change in our thinking. Around the turn of the last century, the focus was on preventing and treating infectious diseases. As a result, doctors discovered the benefits of vaccines and medications to help them achieve these goals. Now, however, the leading cause of illness and death in pets is not infectious disease but chronic, degenerative problems such as cancer and kidney failure. Immune diseases are also occurring with increased frequency. As a result, the focus is slowly shifting among conventional doctors from infectious disease to these degenerative organ and immune problems.

Holistic, integrative doctors are leading the way in this paradigm shift. We are focusing on total pet care, looking at diet, environment, exercise, and supplementation to improve the health of the pet, and decreasing the use of chemicals and conventional medications when possible to try to minimize the incidence of these degenerative and immune disorders.

I wrote *8 Weeks to a Healthy Dog* to help pet owners and doctors adapt to this new way of thinking. If we must shift our focus from "treating disease" to "healing pets," I wanted to find a simple, effective, and—when possible—less expensive approach to achieve our goals. The 8 Weeks to a Healthy Dog Program, which was inspired by a similar program for people developed by integrative human medical doctor Andrew Weil (author of *8 Weeks to Optimum Health*), will help you do just that. By following this program, you will do everything possible to achieve optimum health for your dog.

It has been my experience that owners who follow the steps in this program truly have healthier pets, and they are often able to decrease the ultimate cost of pet health care. I invite you to try the program and would love to hear your results!

Shawn Messonnier, D.V.M.
naturalvet@juno.com

PART ONE

GETTING STARTED

Why a Holistic Approach Is Best for Your Dog

B efore getting into the 8 Weeks to a Healthy Dog Program, I'd like to share with you my thoughts on this holistic/integrative approach. Once you understand how and why it's different from conventional medicine, I think the value of the 8-Week Program will become apparent.

THE VALUE OF CONVENTIONAL TREATMENT

When it comes to pet care, there are two basic schools of thought. First, we have the Western or conventional approach. This is most likely the approach your doctor uses. Like me, most veterinarians are trained at veterinary schools that emphasize a conventional approach to medicine. With this approach, the doctor is trained to properly diagnose and treat disease in your dog. The conventional approach begins with an examination of the pet and questioning of the pet owner in an attempt to take a thorough history. Often, due to rushed, overbooked schedules, the doctor trained in the conventional approach may hurry through this part of the diagnostic process. This rushed approach means that an entire health history is impossible to attain, which may cause the dog's care to suffer as a result.

Following the examination and patient history, conventional diagnostic testing may be necessary. This testing allows the doctor to obtain more information to help him or her make a diagnosis and select the proper therapy. Commonly used conventional diagnostic tests include blood and urine testing, cultures, x-rays, electrocardio-grams, ultrasound tests, biopsies, and CT or MRI scans. Following the tests, the cause of most illnesses becomes apparent, allowing the doctor to select the proper therapy. Most conventional therapies are limited to surgery, radiation therapy, and drug therapy. The most commonly used (and I would argue overused) medications include antibiotics such as amoxicillin and enrofloxacin, non-steroidal anti-inflammatory agents such as Rimadyl and EtoGesic, corticosteroids such as prednisone and prednisolone, and antihistamines such as diphenhydramine and hydroxyzine.

I'm not saying that this conventional or Western approach is ei-ther good or bad; it's simply the approach most doctors use. The focus is on treating disease. Conventional medicine has many posi-tive aspects. For example, surgery is often necessary to save life and cure disease. If your pet has a broken leg, acupuncture will not heal this affliction (although it can be used in the healing process fol-lowing proper surgical stabilization). Likewise, if your dog is bleeding to death, a conventional approach—a blood transfusion—is needed. No herb or homeopathic remedy will save a dog that is in imminent danger of bleeding to death (although herbs and homeo-pathics may assist the pet's recovery following proper conventional medical treatment). Therefore, as you delve into *8 Weeks to a Healthy Dog*, let's not forget the benefits that can come with proper and responsible use of conventional therapies.

THE HOLISTIC APPROACH

The opposite approach is a non-conventional approach. Many call this an Eastern approach, as this is the approach used by doctors out-side of the Western hemisphere (the Orient, India, etc.). Unlike the Western or conventional approach, this system is focused on healing the patient rather than treating the disease. This system is not simply concerned with the physical aspects of the patient, but also with the spiritual and emotional aspects. (I'll admit, it's more difficult to deal with the spiritual and emotional aspects of a pet! However, in using the Eastern approach to heal a pet, we try to make the environment of the pet as wholesome and healthy as possible through behavior modification and various herbs and flower essences. Additionally, helping the pet owner heal his or her own emotional and spiritual side has positive aspects for the pet.)

Like the Western approach, holistic veterinarians perform a full physical examination and take a thorough history. Usually much more time is spent on this aspect of the visit than with the Western approach. Doctors with an Eastern philosophy know that the body can give us a lot of clues to help us determine what is wrong with it.

The Health-Care Triangle

There are three factors involved in properly treating your dog: you, your dog's veterinarian, and your dog. All three are equally important in obtaining the proper diagnosis and treatment. While most people focus on the doctor's role, it is important not to underestimate the role the dog owner has in the dog's health care. When a dog comes in to my office, I totally depend on the information the pet owner provides during the history. The owner's observations of the dog's normal and abnormal behaviors are critical in allowing me to formulate a possible diagnosis and to decide which laboratory tests to run.

One important task for you as the owner is to pick the best doctor you feel comfortable with for your dog. How much you can afford to do for your pet, as well as how easily you can administer the prescribed therapy, are also important in determining your pet's response to treatment.

Finally, the role of your dog is also a factor in the success of the health-care plan. If your dog won't let you give him the prescribed therapy, the chances of successful treatment will be reduced. If your pet won't eat the prescribed diet, this may also reduce the possibility of successful treatment. Don't forget the importance of your role, and share with your pet's doctor any problems you may have in treating your dog. Never be shy about saying "I tried to do it, and I just can't." Your veterinarian will work with you to choose an easier alternative.

Rushing through this aspect of the visit would cause us to overlook important information that can help us achieve the proper diagnosis and treatment. One thing I have learned since incorporating this Eastern approach in my practice is that the dog's body and the owner's astute observations add volumes of information to the database I need in order to get the diagnosis. After prescribing what I believe is the proper therapy, I teach the owners to listen to their pet's body to determine the success or failure of the therapy.

An excellent example of this is the approach to the dog with allergies who likely has terribly itchy skin. I use a variety of herbs, proper diet, and regular bathing with hypoallergenic shampoos and conditioning rinses. Because allergies are genetic diseases, I can't cure my allergic patients. There is simply no way to change a pet's DNA or alter his genetic makeup, so we have to manage the allergies and minimize the allergic response that causes the dog to itch and develop secondary bacterial and yeast infections. Even with the proven therapies I use, many of these dogs will still need some conventional medications (usually steroids) at times of the year when their allergies flare up. By using the Eastern approach, I teach the owners the signs to look for in their dogs before using the steroids. In other words, I tell the owners that their pets' bodies will tell them when it's time to use steroids and when it's time to stop the medicine. Unlike the Western or conventional approach, which might dictate a certain prescribed period of time for drug therapy based on pharmacological research, the Eastern or non-conventional approach treats the dog as the dog's body dictates. We use drugs as needed to heal the pet rather than simply to treat a disease. This is a new approach for many of you, but believe me when I say it is a powerful approach that has proven itself for thousands of years.

With the Eastern approach, a different regimen of diagnostic testing is used than in a Western approach. A purely Eastern practitioner will not rely on conventional testing like blood or urine tests. Instead, the Eastern practitioner looks for physical clues from the dog's body. For example, the Eastern doctor might look at the color of a dog's tongue as well as any saliva adhering to it to obtain certain clues about the illness. Feeling the pulse of the dog gives more information than simply the heart rate. Looking at the color of the sclera (the white part of the eye) may also give the Eastern practitioner a clue as to the patient's medical condition.

Muscle testing, which is called applied kinesiology, is a popular non-conventional test that many holistic practitioners use. This relies on testing various muscle groups for strength or weakness to allow the doctor to pinpoint the problem. Chiropractors commonly use applied kinesiology to help them determine which vertebral segments are out of alignment and require adjustment.

Applied kinesiology can even be used to determine the proper therapy for a particular dog. For example, one dog that is determined to have a bladder problem using applied kinesiology might be treated with the herb uva ursi, whereas another dog with a similar problem might be treated with the homeopathic remedy Cantharis. While both pets may have the same problem, each may require a different therapy as determined by applied kinesiology.

While not all integrative doctors use these Eastern diagnostic tests, the integrative doctors usually use a greater range of testing to diagnose the sick dog than their Western counterparts.

The Personalized Approach

An extremely important aspect of the holistic approach is for doctors to personalize the therapy for the dog based upon our diagnostic testing as just mentioned. Let's use the example of allergies to show the difference in treatment between a conventional approach and a holistic approach. If you take your allergic dog to a conventional doctor, the treatment options for allergies are limited. The conventional doctor might use shampoo and fatty acid therapy. (Fatty acid therapy was once considered a non-conventional therapy, but thankfully most conventional doctors are now incorporating its use in the

How to Find a Holistic Veterinarian

Despite the fact that many dog owners are interested in a holistic approach to pet care, there are really very few holistic veterinarians. Finding one to care for your dog can be challenging. Keep in mind that many holistic veterinarians offer phone consultations for people who do not live close by. Of course, it's always ideal for a veterinarian to see a pet and perform a physical examination. But I have done many successful phone consultations with pet owners seeking a holistic approach to pet care. If you decide to go this route, you will still need your conventional veterinarian to run tests and offer any conventional therapies that may be needed. The holistic veterinarian can make recommendations and mail herbs, homeopathic remedies, and supplements to you if you can't buy them locally.

Despite the challenge of finding a holistic veterinarian, I believe without question that it is worth the time and effort. Holistic veterinarians' whole approach to medical care is quite different from that of conventional veterinarians. In general, holistic doctors are more interested in healing pets rather than treating diseases. A holistic veterinarian should look at your dog as a "whole dog," not just as the source of a specific problem or symptom. Having a holistic attitude means that doctors and owners don't just focus on the problem at hand; instead, they look at total wellness for the pet.

Another difference between conventional medicine and holistic medicine is that while conventional medicine usually focuses on *treating* diseases, the goal of holistic pet care is to *prevent* disease in the first place. We strive to keep dogs well, rather than just treating them when they are sick. Because of this, you can begin a holistic approach to pet care the moment you get your puppy or dog.

Here are some tips for finding a holistic veterinarian:

treatment regimen.) But most commonly, a conventional doctor will use a corticosteroid such as prednisone or an antihistamine such as diphenhydramine. The dog will get better for a short period of time, then relapse, at which point the drugs will be prescribed again, possibly at an even higher dosage.

Now let's look at the treatment of this same allergic dog using a holistic approach. If medicines are necessary to make the pet com-

- **Check with other pet owners you trust.** A recommendation and referral are the best ways to find a doctor. If you get a referral, it's still wise to visit the doctor yourself when your dog has a minor problem or simply for a checkup and nutritional consultation to make sure you like the doctor and staff.
- **Check the Yellow Pages and other phone books.** While I don't advertise in phone books, some holistic doctors do. If you find one, set up a time to talk with the doctor so you can be sure you like him or her and would trust him or her with your dog's care.
- **Check with local health and natural food stores.** My practice gets a lot of referrals from these sources. Most stores maintain a list of holistic dentists, doctors, and veterinarians. Even with a referral from the store, you should still visit with the doctor, because you still need to get to know the doctor and feel comfortable with his or her approach.
- **Check the Internet.** The official group of holistic veterinarians, the American Holistic Veterinary Medical Association, maintains a Web site, www.altvetmed.com, that lists its members by city and state. If you don't have Internet access, you can call them at (410) 569-0795. Finding a doctor this way is no guarantee that you will like the doctor, so you'll still have to follow up with a phone call or personal visit. But finding a veterinarian this way does at least ensure that your doctor wants to stay current with the information in this growing field.

By choosing a holistic veterinarian for your pet, adopting a holistic attitude yourself, and following the simple steps presented here in *8 Weeks to a Healthy Dog,* you will be taking important steps to prevent disease and heal your dog if he becomes ill.

fortable, the holistic doctor may use the same prescribed dosage (although he or she will use the pet's response to the drug to tell when to stop treatment, rather than giving it for a certain amount of time simply based on a recommended treatment time). The holistic veterinarian may instead use applied kinesiology to determine the proper dosage and treatment regimen.

The holistic doctor also has many more therapies available for treating the pet. These can include acupuncture, homeopathy, herbs, diet, nutritional supplements, ayurvedic, chiropractic, magnetic, flower essence, TTouch, and essential oil therapy. He or she can use any of these therapies (picking the best therapies for each case based on personal experience, or once again by using applied kinesiology) to help the pet heal, and observe the dog's response to determine the proper dosage and treatment interval.

This approach, which relies heavily on owner involvement and observation, is a very personal—and holistic—approach that does what is best for the dog and focuses on healing the pet, not simply treating the disease.

Holistic versus Alternative: What's in a Name?

Holistic medicine is the term favored by many doctors. The international organization of veterinarians who practice a non-conventional approach is called the American Holistic Veterinary Medical Association (AHVMA). Their Web site is www.altvetmed.com. Holistic, occasionally spelled wholistic, refers to two things. First, holistic refers to the whole pet. Being a holistic doctor, I don't simply focus on the problem at hand but on the whole pet. If an owner brings in his or her dog for allergies, I also focus on the pet's overall health. My physical examination focuses on other organ systems, such as the heart, urogenital system, lungs, liver, gastrointestinal system (including the teeth and gums), and nervous system. I want to know about the pet's diet and vaccination history, and if the dog is currently taking any medications. I always question the owners at length.

As you can see, this focus on the whole pet is different from the focus so often seen in a conventional practice where the doctor may tend to focus only on the problem at hand. The holistic focus allows us to concentrate on healing the "whole" pet rather than simply treating the "diseased part." Second, by being holistic, I can offer a "whole" array of treatment options, both conventional and non-conventional. This doubles my choice of therapies and my chance of helping each pet.

Other terms often used to describe this holistic or Eastern approach include alternative medicine, complementary medicine, natural medicine, and integrative medicine. I'll explain each of these in detail.

The term "alternative" simply means "something else." So calling the non-conventional approach **alternative medicine** means that we choose to use some alternative therapy rather than a conventional therapy. Most holistic doctors don't like the term alternative medicine. With rare exceptions, doctors like me don't choose a treatment as an alternative to a conventional therapy. Usually we will combine a conventional therapy, when appropriate, with a non-conventional one. We don't consider our therapies alternatives because we don't want to turn our backs on conventional medicine when conventional medicine can help our patients.

Now, there are some doctors and some clients who confuse the term "holistic" with "alternative" and have very closed minds when it comes to *any* type of conventional therapy. I've had more than one client get upset with me when I recommended a conventional treatment and that client thought I was a "holistic" doctor. While "alternative" therapies can be quite helpful—and may even be better choices than conventional therapies in some cases—I would never ignore the possibility of using a conventional therapy if I thought this type of therapy would help my patient. Doing so would not only be closed-minded and ignorant but malpractice!

There are certainly closed-minded doctors and pet owners. Some are closed-minded to any type of therapy that does not fall under the "conventional" heading, and some are closed-minded to any type of conventional therapy. Unfortunately this closed-mindedness can harm and even kill our dogs. (See "On the Case with Dr. Shawn: Katie" on page 12 for a sad example.) My goal for you and your dog

(continued on page 14)

On the Case with Dr. Shawn

KATIE

Let me share a sad story of what happens when someone who is interested in "alternative" therapies becomes closed-minded to conventional medicine. I was contacted by a husband and wife who owned a sweet little dog named Katie. Katie was a seven-year-old West Highland white terrier ("Westie"). She had been diagnosed by another veterinarian with a type of cancer called lymphosarcoma (also called lymphoma). This type of cancer is quite common in dogs. It usually affects middle-aged and older dogs, but unfortunately we are now seeing this cancer occur in younger dogs as well. (Some dogs are even less than one year old!)

There are several forms of lymphosarcoma; Katie had the most common form, in which her lymph nodes painlessly enlarged. Her owners sought out my advice, since they wanted to avoid conventional cancer therapies and try a non-conventional approach. After reviewing her medical record and biopsy results, I agreed with the original veterinarian's diagnosis of lymphosarcoma. While this type of cancer cannot usually be cured (regardless of the therapy chosen), it is quite treatable. Many pets with this form of lymphosarcoma live 12 to 18 months or longer with chemotherapy. Therefore, it is usually a very rewarding cancer to treat. Most dogs do quite well with chemotherapy, and they rarely experience any of the side effects that are so well known in people treated with chemotherapy, such as lack of appetite, hair loss, and vomiting.

I explained to Katie's owners that the best approach would be to combine chemotherapy with herbs, homeopathy, and nutritional supplements. The chemotherapy would quickly put Katie in remission and shrink her swollen lymph nodes back to their normal size. The non-conventional therapies would boost her immune system (something the chemotherapy would actually suppress), helping her body fight the cancer as well. Additionally, some types of herbs and nutritional supplements can minimize the side effects of chemotherapy, and some supplements such as antioxidants may increase the effectiveness of the chemotherapy (while also minimizing the toxicity from the cancer-fighting drugs).

Unfortunately, Katie's owners were totally opposed to using any conventional drugs to treat Katie. The husband was a cancer survivor who related horror stories of side effects he suffered during treatment for his cancer. Despite my explanation that side effects from chemotherapy are very rare in pets, he was not moved. He was so against using chemotherapy that he told me that if he ever had cancer again he would refuse to undergo another round of chemotherapy.

I then asked them if we could use prednisone, a corticosteroid, to help Katie. Prednisone is one of the chemotherapy drugs used to treat pets with lymphosarcoma. It makes the dog feel better, increases appetite, and quickly kills many cancerous lymphoblasts, shrinking lymph nodes to a more normal size. Katie's owners were also opposed to using prednisone. Simply put, they wanted no drugs and only "alternatives." I therefore prescribed several remedies, including herbs, homeopathics, and nutritional supplements. I carefully explained to Katie's owners that I did not hold out a lot of hope for Katie, as my experience with using only supplements to help treat cancer has not been positive. I don't consider the supplements I recommend for pets with cancer an "alternative" as Katie's owners did, but rather as an important part of the total healing process. But I wanted to help Katie, and I always believe that doing something is better than doing nothing. I sent Katie and her owners home with the treatment regimen, hoping for the best.

Two weeks later, the husband and wife returned with Katie, who was now very sick. It was obvious that she had not improved with the "alternative" regimen but had actually worsened, as the cancerous lymph cells had spread through her body. The owners did not want to see Katie suffer, so I agreed with their decision to perform euthanasia and end her life.

This story still bothers me as I share it with you. There was no reason for Katie to have died so soon with lymphosarcoma. Even with only using prednisone, she had the chance to live three to six months. But the closed-minded approach of her owners, who were opposed to helping Katie with conventional medicine, resulted in a death that I still feel was way too premature.

as you get involved with your own 8-Week Program is to be open-minded so that you and your doctor can choose whatever type of therapy is best for your pet.

Complementary medicine is another phrase commonly used to describe a non-conventional approach. This phrase, which is currently favored by many doctors, implies that our non-conventional approach "complements" conventional treatments. The complementary treatment is viewed not as an alternative but as an adjunct to improve the dog's chance of healing when the appropriate conventional therapy is used.

Natural medicine is another commonly used phrase. The term "natural" implies "from nature," as opposed to "chemically" created therapies. Naturopathic doctors prefer herbs to conventional drugs, as they believe that something created by nature is less toxic and better for the pet. In simple terms, naturopaths believe that a natural treatment is, well, natural! Anything that is natural must be okay, right? Well, in general, this may be true, but anything can be toxic if the dose is high enough! Certain herbs, such as ephedra, black walnut, comfrey, and wormwood are certainly natural, but there are some conventional drugs that are actually safer than these potent herbs for general use. In general, I like natural therapies, but as with conventional drugs, I exercise caution when using anything that is potent enough to cause a change and healing in the body.

Like my human-medicine counterpart Dr. Andrew Weil, and many of my colleagues in the AHVMA, I prefer the phrase **integrative medicine**. This approach allows the doctor to combine the best that both the conventional approach and the non-conventional approach offer. I like to think of an integrative approach as allowing me

DR. SHAWN SAYS

Healing your pet rather than simply treating problems is our goal.

twice as many treatment (or healing) options. In other words, I'm not restricted to just surgery, radiation therapy, and chemotherapy. While a conventional doctor has nothing more to offer than these three therapies, by offering an integrative approach, I have many more options and am not limited in my treatment of the pet. In some instances, such as liver disease and certain cancers, there may not be any conventional therapy that can be used. In these situations, the number of therapies an integrative approach offers is quite helpful and, in some instances, it can be lifesaving.

Regardless of what you decide to call it, keep in mind that *healing*, rather than simply *treating*, is our goal. While it is true that sometimes the best we can hope for is treating the disease to make a terminally ill pet comfortable until death inevitably takes over, in most cases we want the pet's body to heal so that the disease will not take over the body or continue to reoccur. As Dr. Weil notes in his wonderful book *8 Weeks to Optimum Health*, healing comes from within the body, relying on the body's innate ability to seek health. Treatment comes from outside, where we artificially do something to the body. The goal of healing is permanent health (though it isn't always attainable), whereas the goal of treatment is to make the disease go away until the next illness occurs.

MAKING THE BEST CHOICE FOR YOUR DOG

Everyone must choose the type of health care he or she wants for his or her dog. Similarly, veterinarians must choose the type of health care they offer their patients. This decision, I believe, is the one thing that determines the quality of life a pet will have, and it is the most important decision the pet owner and veterinarian can make. Just as I made the decision for "healing care" and a "holistic/integrative" approach, you are now being given the opportunity to make a similar decision. You have so much power over the type of health care your

On the Case with Dr. Shawn

BUDDY

My motto in my veterinary practice is that we offer "Hope for the Hopeless." I see so many ill pets who have been labeled "hopeless" by their veterinarians. Not satisfied with this label, their owners seek my advice for a second opinion. Until I started offering holistic/integrative care, I had no idea how many doctors were giving up on their patients. Amazingly, more than 50 percent of the pets I now see who have been labeled "hopeless" by their doctors are not even very sick! Many of these pets have been incorrectly diagnosed, or correctly diagnosed but with a hopeless prognosis. This case demonstrates my frustration with this "hopeless" prognosis.

Buddy is a five-year-old male beagle. He was diagnosed by his prior veterinarian as having acute kidney failure and treated for several days. On Friday of the week of his diagnosis, his veterinarian gave up hope, since the results of Buddy's blood tests were still abnormal. His owners told me that they were told by the veterinarian that nothing more could be done for Buddy. They were told to take him home over the weekend, spend some time with him, and prepare to return on Monday to say goodbye to Buddy and have him euthanized.

When I saw Buddy on Monday, his owners were obviously not prepared to euthanize him. I reviewed Buddy's laboratory results and saw that, even though the kidney enzymes in his blood were elevated, they really weren't that bad. I was also struck by how healthy Buddy looked. Dogs with acute kidney failure are usually very sick and quite literally dying in front of me. Buddy's owners stated that Buddy never really acted that sick, and because of this they had a hard time coming to grips with their veterinarian's recommendation to have Buddy euthanized. I agreed with them that euthanasia was totally unnecessary. Over the next few months, we successfully treated Buddy and lowered his kidney enzymes, and he is doing great at this time. The value of a second opinion and a round of non-conventional therapies gave Buddy's owners "Hope for the Hopeless."

In some cases, of course, the dogs really are quite ill, and conventional medicine truly has no hope for these pets. That's why I like the integrative approach: My options are unlimited, and many pets that can't be helped with conventional medicine can be helped by the other therapies I have in my treatment arsenal.

pet will receive! The 8 Weeks to a Healthy Dog Program seeks to offer your pet the best care possible. By reading this book and making the decision to try the 8-Week Program, you have chosen health and healing for your pet. Using this program will give you the edge that you need to have as healthy a dog as possible.

Selecting a type of health care is very much a personal choice. For those of us who have chosen an integrated approach, combining the best of conventional medicine with the best of "natural" therapies, the road began with a search for "something more" that conventional medicine was not able to offer. By reading this book, my guess is that you, too, are looking for that "something more" for your dog. Maybe you're fed up with conventional medicine (as is the case with some of my clients). Maybe you simply want something different for your pet, something that can be more positive (healing the pet versus treating disease), something that is often much less toxic than conventional therapies, and something that is usually less expensive over the life of your pet.

One very important example is choosing the best diet for your pet. After reading "Week 3: Choosing the Best Diet for Your Dog" on page 73, you'll no longer have to feed your dog processed foods, which contain potentially harmful chemicals, additives, and byproducts. Instead, you'll know how to read pet food labels and select the healthiest diet for your pet. Or even better, you can use the recipes in the book to prepare nutritious, fresh meals for your dog right at home.

Another benefit to choosing a holistic health-care program for your dog is minimizing unnecessary vaccination. Part of my goal of changing the way we care for our dogs is to reduce the frequency of vaccinations. Many dogs receive repeated immunizations despite the fact that most pets do not need these shots. Instead, owners should rely on vaccine titers (antibody levels) and let the pets' bodies determine which vaccines, if any, are needed.

Hope for the Hopeless

You may be wondering why I began my search for "something better," and why I feel the need to share what I've found with readers around the globe.

To start with, I had to admit something that was a bit uncomfortable. Even though I felt that I was a good doctor when I began my search, I was forced to admit that there had to be more than simply what I was already doing for my patients. While I had been trained to be a good "treater" of disease, I had to face the fact that I was not a good "healer." Only when I admitted that I needed to become a healer rather than a treater could I face my shortcomings and search for something better.

Once I found this great new world of natural therapies, I started seeing positive results in my patients, many of whom I had not been able to help with only conventional medicine. As a result, my motto became "Hope for the Hopeless." No longer did I have to tell a dog owner that I couldn't help his pet, because now I had many more treatment options available.

Not wanting to be selfish with this newfound knowledge that gave hope and healing to many dog owners, I wanted to find a vehicle to share my excitement. That's when my publishers and editors agreed to work with me to share my story and vision.

As a result of my writing, including the book you are now reading, and works by other forward-looking veterinarians like Dr. Richard Pitcairn's groundbreaking *Complete Guide to Natural Health for Dogs and Cats,* I'm excited to say that we are already changing the way pet owners and veterinarians are treating and caring for pets. No longer are pets considered hopeless just because conventional medicine can't offer help.

With the thoroughly researched therapies I've presented in my articles and books, pet owners can learn to "just say no to drugs" for their pets and instead rely on natural, healing therapies whenever possible. Instead of covering up symptoms and treating disease, veterinarians can now heal pets and create true health. I invite you to share this incredible health-care choice and journey with me!

I discuss this in more detail in "Week 1: The Veterinary Visit" on page 29.

You'll also discover plenty of alternatives to conventional medications. While conventional medications can be used safely and correctly in our 8-Week Program, there are many instances when safer and less expensive alternatives exist. For example, arthritis is best treated with glucosamine, chondroitin, or hyaluronic acid rather than non-steroidal medications. Allergies are best treated with herbs, supplements, diets, and bathing, with minimal need for corticosteroids.

ASK DR. SHAWN

Dear Dr. Shawn: "Do these unconventional therapies really work?"

A: Actually, I'm asked this question a lot. And the follow-up question always seems to be, "What proof do I have that shows they are as effective as conventional medicines?"

To answer your first question, do these therapies work, I can only respond with a definite "Yes." Most of these therapies are not new. Homeopathy has been used for over 100 years—longer than conventional drugs—and acupuncture and herbal remedies have been used for several *thousands* of years!

To answer your second question, I can also state unequivocally that I have seen proof firsthand that the therapies I choose to help heal my patients do work. If they didn't work, I would find something else that did! Why continue prescribing a therapy that fails to result in patient improvement? Certainly my practice would not get the number of referrals from satisfied clients it does if my patients didn't improve. I see so many patients because I choose therapies that effectively solve problems for pet owners, and because there is a general dissatisfaction among these pet owners with the lack of effectiveness of supposedly "proven" conventional therapies. The effectiveness of the therapies I use is the reason that I continue to see new clients who want to begin healing their pets rather than simply treating diseases.

Cognitive disorder, often called "doggie Alzheimer's disease," is best treated with choline, lecithin, or ginkgo, which are much less expensive than conventional medication.

Using the information in *8 Weeks to a Healthy Dog*, you can begin to take a holistic approach to your pet's care. By taking a holistic approach and listening to your dog's body, you and your veterinarian can fine-tune any therapy needed. This holistic approach allows true healing rather than simply treating a disease. And this is what natural pet care is all about!

An Overview of
the 8-Week Program

Take a good look at your dog. Does he look healthy? My guess is your answer is a cheerful "yes." By all appearances, most dogs *look* healthy. It's been my experience, too, that all pet owners like to think that their dogs are healthy. But sadly, the truth is that many of these dogs are just surviving. But here's the great news: It's not such a long trip between surviving and thriving. In fact, you, me, and your dog are going to take this trip together—in just eight short weeks!

In this chapter, I'd like to give you an overview of the 8 Weeks to a Healthy Dog Program. Consider this a map of the journey we're about to take. I'll explain my reasoning for why we're about to spend this time together and talk you through the eight weeks.

DOES *MY* DOG NEED THIS PROGRAM?

Even though your dog may look, and even seem, healthy, there are many things you can do to make him even healthier and prevent health problems in the future. Just by picking up this book and embarking on this program, you and your dog are ahead of so many others I see.

Some dogs do not receive annual veterinary care, so detection of harmful or fatal illnesses is not possible until it is too late. Other dogs do go to the veterinarian once a year. Unfortunately, their doctors do not believe in total health care. Instead, they focus on vaccinations that may or may not be necessary for these dogs. The sad irony is that they may contribute to early illness and death in some pets.

Still other dogs receive an annual physical exam, but their doctors don't notice health problems such as periodontal disease, heart disease, and skin tumors. Or if a problem is diagnosed, some owners choose not to treat the problem until it worsens.

Many dogs in our society are fed nutritionally inadequate generic pet foods, chosen because of an inexpensive price or fancy advertisement. Years ago I heard a story about how cereals made and advertised for children were often less nutritious than the boxes they came in! Because of federal regulations, cereals now provide some of the necessary nutrients for people. I wish the same could be said of all dog foods.

Many dogs don't get any exercise. As a result, they become obese. Obesity is the number-one nutritional disease in dogs, as it is in people. Other dogs lack the muscle tone that is so obvious in their wild canine relatives. When these dogs are forced to run or play, they tire easily from lack of regular exercise, inadequate nutrition, and a very marginal state of health.

Some dogs are infested with internal or external parasites, or both. Because of the life cycles of some of these parasites, owners and doctors are often unaware of their existence. Yet your dog knows about them. He's not able to function fully because these parasites are robbing him of vital nutrients and an adequate blood supply!

I don't want any of these things to happen to your dog. I want—and I know you do, too—so much more for your beloved pet. And with my simple, inexpensive, and healthy program, together we will help your dog enjoy a long, healthy, happy life. While some doctors estimate the average dog lives to be 8 to 10 years old, we know that most truly healthy dogs can live more than 15 years. Certainly there are no guarantees, but investing just eight weeks could almost double your dog's life!

That is what *8 Weeks to a Healthy Dog* is all about.

WHY 8 WEEKS?

I believe that dog health programs should be easy and affordable. In my practice, I've worked with dog owners to make their dog's care just that. But after reading Dr. Andrew Weil's wonderful book *8 Weeks to Optimum Health*, I wondered if there was a similar program I could offer my patients. Since I was not aware of such a simple but successful preventive program for pets, I decided to create one.

In each of the next eight weeks, I'll take you through a different health-care topic designed to improve your dog's life and his standard of care. While you certainly could do everything at once, I think the 8-Week Program makes sense. Here are three good reasons:

First, it's much easier for all of us to make changes slowly, in small bites. Like me, most of you probably have limited time, so each week I'll just be asking you to make a small time commitment. Plus, dogs are creatures of habit, kind of like people. They do best with small changes.

Second, establishing true health takes time. You can't make the types of changes we'll be making in your dog's life—to his diet, exercise, grooming, and more—by waving a magic wand. It also takes time to see results. But you *will* see them! Since it often takes four to eight weeks to see changes, the 8-Week time period gives enough time for owners to make changes and allows time to see results.

Finally, even these simple, healthy changes can cost money. Tackling one health-care issue each week will allow you to break up and spread out the cost of doing the program into eight separate payments. But the program is not typically expensive. And the money that you spend will pay off in the long run because having a healthier dog will reduce your health-care costs over the life of your pet.

I believe following a program like *8 Weeks to a Healthy Dog* will ultimately be less expensive and healthier for a dog than treating diseases as they occur. I also believe this program is truly holistic because it is adaptable to your needs and the needs of your dog. Personalized pet care is the goal of the 8 Weeks to a Healthy Dog Program. This means that you can tackle health-care issues as you find the time and can afford to do so. Taking this personalized approach is new to most dog owners. Most owners find this approach, where they take the lead in their dogs' care, very refreshing and liberating.

While the structure of the 8-Week Program is set up so that each important aspect of health care is dealt with during its own week, feel free to adapt the program to fit your needs. In my practice, the program is actually quite informal now that I have been following it for several years. My clients and I often cover several topics in one week rather than using the 8-Week structure I've suggested in this book, and that's worked fine, too.

Plus, while there are goals for you to meet each week, nothing takes place in a vacuum. For example, during Week 1 you'll take your dog to the veterinarian for an exam and tests. Later in the program, we'll talk about having any diseases the exam turns up corrected. But, of course, there's nothing to stop you from having a problem fixed earlier! Don't let the structure of the 8-Week Program tie your hands when it comes to common sense and good health care.

This program is for you and your dog. Please adapt it so that it serves you best.

WEEK-BY-WEEK PREVIEW

Here's a preview of what we'll be doing in the next eight weeks to get your dog in the best health of his life.

Week 1: In the first week, you'll take your dog to the veterinarian for a thorough physical exam and lab tests. This is a critical first step toward good health for your dog. I'll offer tips on how to find a good veterinarian and be a good owner. I'll explain what you should expect from your dog's veterinarian visit and discuss the controversy surrounding vaccinations. This chapter will help you to shift your thinking away from conventional medicine's emphasis on drugs and vaccines and instead focus on our holistic program. This chapter will save you time and money as it optimizes your dog's veterinarian visits and prevents expensive health problems in the future.

Week 2: This week, we'll do our best to control a common problem in pets: parasites. Many dogs harbor internal or external parasites that weaken them and may cause serious diseases, yet the owner may not notice. And when you consider that the dog can transmit many parasites to the family, parasite control takes on even greater importance. I'll describe the most common parasites here and offer dozens of tips to free your dog and environment of these pesky bugs.

Week 3: In Week 3, we'll find the right diet for your dog. Of the dozens of commercial diets available, a few are good, but some are downright terrible and unhealthy. This week, I'll arm you with the information you need to make the best choices about your dog's food. You'll learn which type of diet is best. (Hint: It's *not* the most expensive!) We'll also talk about healthy treats to give your dog. Plus, I'll share my own recipe for the very best homemade diet to feed to your dog. Your dog will eat it up!

Week 4: Almost midway through our program, in Week 4 we'll begin supplementing your pet's diet. Because no dog's diet is perfect, all dogs benefit from nutritional supplements, such as plant enzymes, super green foods, omega-3 fatty acids, vitamins, and minerals. This week, I'll explain why your dog needs supplements, talk about the most common supplements for dogs, give you my supplement shopping list, and tell you which supplements can comfort and heal your dog if he gets sick.

Week 5: This week, we're going to treat any diseases discovered during your dog's Week 1 veterinarian visit. Most owners don't realize it, but the majority of "healthy" pets I see have at least one disease that may cause pain and overall poor health. For example, periodontal disease affects more than 99 percent of the new dogs I see in my practice. In this chapter, I'll talk about the most common dog diseases, describe the conventional treatments for them, and offer many healthy, holistic alternatives.

Week 6: This week, we'll get your dog on a sound, healthy exercise program. Exercise will improve your dog's physical and mental health. And, if you work out with your dog, you may be surprised at how much better *you'll* look and feel, too! Owners often report that this is the most fun part of the 8 Weeks to a Healthy Dog Program. I'll explain why your dog should be exercising, how much is enough, and which types are best. Plus, we'll talk about exercises for dogs with special needs, such as those with behavior problems, heart disease, or obesity. We'll also talk about three alternatives to exercise: massage, acupressure, and TTouch.

Week 7: In the homestretch now, this week we'll try to wean your pet off potentially harmful drugs, including antibiotics, corticosteroids, and non-steroidal anti-inflammatory medications. I am convinced that many pets are in poor health as a result of excessive and inappropriate use of drugs. While drug therapy is often necessary and in some instances can save the life of a dog, when medications are used incorrectly they can cause harm. This week, I'll help you say "no" to drugs for your dog. We'll talk about the three most commonly misused drugs, and I'll offer dozens of natural alternatives to them.

Week 8: Finally, in Week 8, we'll place your dog on a regular grooming program to minimize future problems with his coat, ears, skin, and teeth. I'll tell you about the best bathing, brushing, nail care, and ear care. By the end of our 8-Week Program, from nose to tail, your dog will look better—and feel better, too!

WRAPPING UP

As we start out on our 8-Week journey, I encourage you to use this program in conjunction with sound veterinary advice. Work with your dog's health-care provider to maximize the program. If your doctor is opposed to some of the ideas in the program, find someone who will work with you to allow your dog to receive the health care to which he's entitled. Nothing in this program is "far out" or "wacky." Instead, it follows logic and sound medical advice. *8 Weeks to a Healthy Dog* presents a simple program for you to do your best to help ensure maximum health for your dog.

If you're ready to get started, let's go!

PART TWO

THE

8-WEEK

PROGRAM

3

WEEK 1:
The Veterinary Visit

The first week of our healthy dog program begins where it should, with a visit to your veterinarian's office. Before we can prescribe what's best for your dog, we must know what kind of shape he's in at the start of our program.

I know that many owners (and unfortunately some doctors) take the attitude that "He looks healthy, so he must be okay." Nothing could be further from the truth! I examine numerous animals each year that look healthy but have one or more illnesses, some of which can be quite serious.

It's been my experience that more than 99 percent of dogs have mild to severe periodontal disease, requiring their teeth to be cleaned under anesthesia at least once a year. Take a moment right now to examine your pet's teeth and gums. Unless your dog has had a recent dental cleaning, my guess is that your "healthy" dog has periodontal disease. The teeth, when healthy and free of infection, are white and the gums are pink (unless you have a dog with pigmented gums such as a Chow Chow). If the teeth have any yellow or brown tartar on them, and if the gum line (the place on the gums where the teeth and gums meet) is reddened—a sign of gingivitis—then your dog has periodontal disease and requires treatment. If your dog has not had a recent dental cleaning, you should schedule one before starting him on our 8 Weeks to a Healthy Dog Program.

Early detection of disease is critical for early treatment and, in many cases, a complete cure. Therefore, we start our 8 Weeks to a Healthy Dog Program with a complete diagnostic evaluation.

On the Case with Dr. Shawn

CHEWY

Sometimes I diagnose diseases that are more serious than peri-odontal disease in healthy-looking pets. For example, I recently examined a young male Shih Tzu named Chewy during his annual visit. The puppy had just turned one year old, so we reviewed with the owner all of the new information she needed for her now-adult dog.

Part of our annual visit is a baseline blood profile, designed to give me all sorts of valuable information about the pet's health, information you and I can't see but still need. As I discussed in "Welcome to Our 8-Week Program" on page ix, I believe some sort of laboratory evaluation such as a blood profile should be a standard part of every pet's annual visit. Most doctors do not include a blood profile for the annual visit, preferring instead to rely on often unnecessary and potentially harmful vaccines to maintain "health." In Chewy's case, this would have been a terrible mistake.

Despite a "healthy" appearance, Chewy's blood profile came back indicating kidney disease. Since this seemed highly unusual in such a young dog, we repeated the blood tests in two weeks. Sure enough, the blood tests came back reinforcing our initial diagnosis of kidney disease, only now the blood tests indicated a worsening of the disease as the kidney enzymes had increased.

Further evaluation and testing indicated that Chewy had an inherited, congenital kidney disorder often seen in Shih Tzus. While we ultimately can't save him, Chewy is currently healthy and on a diet designed to slow down the progression of his kidney disease with appropriate nutritional supplements.

You may be asking how it is possible that Chewy has a fatal disease and still "looks healthy." Looks can be deceiving. At some point in every disease (usually very early in the disease process), every pet looks and acts "healthy" until the disease has progressed to a point where reversing the problem is often impossible. That is why many holistic doctors share my belief (reinforced on a regular basis as we find problems in apparently healthy pets) that every pet needs a complete diagnostic evaluation every year. Remember: Early detection is vital!

Remember that for every year your dog ages, this is the equivalent of your aging about 7 to 10 years. If your dog is only evaluated annually, that is the same as your seeing your doctor once a decade, which is woefully inadequate.

The evaluation should include a thorough physical examination, history, and blood and urine tests. Your doctor should be looking for diseases of the kidney, liver, and heart, as well as various kinds of cancers. In my practice, Paws & Claws Animal Hospital in Plano, Texas, we also find a number of pets with thyroid disease and low platelet or red blood cell counts, so have your dog checked for these problems as well.

WHAT TO EXPECT FROM YOUR DOG'S EXAM

The physical examination must be a thorough examination, not just a routine "quickie" once-over. Here's what I do when I'm giving a physical examination: I listen to the heart and lungs, checking for heart murmurs (which indicate heart disease) and abnormal heart rhythms. I make sure airflow through the lungs and airway structures

DR. SHAWN SAYS

To detect diseases early, before serious problems develop, it's important to do regular diagnostic testing. In most cases, pets without disease can be tested annually until they reach middle to older age. Once pets reach middle to older age (usually seven years of age and older), I think testing every six months is more appropriate. While there is no right or wrong battery of tests, in most cases your veterinarian should do blood and urine testing that will allow him or her to detect problems of the kidneys, liver, red blood cells, white blood cells, pancreas, and thyroid gland. Pets with disease (such as diabetes or kidney disease) will require more frequent laboratory testing to allow monitoring of their diseases.

(bronchi and alveoli) is normal and unobstructed. I look at the skin and ears, checking for evidence of hair loss, infection, inflammation, tumors, and primary skin lesions. I palpate (feel) the abdomen and lymph nodes, checking for organ enlargement and tumors.

I check the dog's mouth, looking for periodontal disease and obvious oral tumors. (Most oral tumors are easier to notice when the pet is anesthetized for a dental cleaning, which is another important reason to have regular dental cleanings performed under anesthesia.) I inspect the eyes for signs of glaucoma, cataracts, cloudiness of the lens, and discoloration, which can indicate anemia or jaundice. I like to watch the dog move, so I can make sure there are no signs of lameness, which can indicate arthritis, bone cysts, infections, or bone tumors.

Taking a good history is also very important in helping me evaluate a pet's health. I depend on my clients to help me during the annual visit. This means they must tell me about any problems they have noticed so I can address them. No matter how thorough I may be, I can and do overlook problems. Therefore, I ask my clients to make a list prior to the visit, noting any concerns they have, so we can discuss these issues during their visits. I encourage you to do the same. Write down anything you have concerns about or any physical problems you may have noticed.

No concern is too minor or too "stupid," so don't be shy. My clients routinely bring up concerns that I need to address. Their concerns show me they truly care about helping their pets, and they want to take an active or even a proactive role in pet care.

A preventive measure we instituted several years ago in my practice is taking an annual blood test from our dog patients. We have had very few owners decline this preventive approach. All of us have become conditioned to have blood tests during our own yearly checkups, so it only makes sense to offer this same level of quality preventive care to our dogs. However, most veterinarians don't insist on taking blood or even offering this service to their clients. One colleague told me over lunch, when discussing the need of an annual blood test to allow for early detection of serious diseases, that his clients "won't go for that." Why not?! My clients go for it—and even demand it!

Finding a Good Veterinarian

I always say that medical care for pets involves a triangle. At one point is the doctor, using all of his or her skills to bring any concerns to light and properly treat them. At point number two in the triangle is the pet, whose body must be healthy and strong enough to heal itself with the doctor's assistance. Point number three in our triangle is you, the owner. No matter how good a doctor your veterinarian might be, and no matter how strong your pet's desire to become "well," we need your help. You must communicate concerns to your veterinarian. You must administer any remedies that are prescribed, and if you can't treat the pet as directed, you must be forthcoming enough to share this.

So many owners really can't communicate with their pets' doctors, and that's too bad. Unless the doctor and owner function as a team, your pet will never attain the level of health that you and I desire. If your doctor is not a member of the team, "trade" him and find someone else. Your doctor, and you, must be dedicated to total holistic pet care. If your doctor would rather treat symptoms (a typical conventional approach) and not prevent problems and establish vibrant good health, your pet will suffer. Good doctors are out there; find one to be a valuable member of your team. Here's how to see how a veterinarian stacks up.

The best doctors are the ones who:

• **Continue their education.** No matter how smart your veterinarian might be, he or she must read journals and attend continuing education meetings whenever practical. Medical knowledge is constantly changing and evolving.

For example, the way I treat my patients changes all the time.

How I approach a certain problem this year may be different from what I did last year. I must be dedicated to my patients and still enjoy the thrill of discovery and learning new, better ways to help pets achieve holistic wellness.

• **Love their job.** Yes, we all have bad days and cases that don't turn out as we hoped. Yet, veterinarians must truly love what they do, or this lack of enthusiasm will hinder their abilities as health-care providers.

When I was asked at my veterinary school interview why I wanted to be a veterinarian, I answered that "I wanted to do something the rest of my life that I enjoyed and could make a decent living doing." Notice that I didn't say that I wanted to be a veterinarian because I "loved animals." This is a ridiculous reason to go into veterinary medicine. And while it is sad that some doctors not only do not love animals but actually dislike them, it should be a given that we all love animals. Notice that money was not my prime motivating factor. Yes, we all would love to make all sorts of money. But as long as I can live comfortably and provide for my family, that's a noble goal.

More important than money, I want to have fun at my career, and that's why I became a veterinarian. For the most part, I have fun at work. I enjoy meeting all sorts of people and their pets, and I am particularly challenged to help those pets other doctors consider "hopeless" cases. While I can't always have a 100 percent success rate, those particularly frustrating cases that I can help let me know that my skills are not wasted, and that I am making a difference in the lives of many pets. If I can keep a pet alive and offer him a good quality life for even just a bit longer, especially if no one else has been able to help a pet, I am truly satisfied.

• **Communicate effectively with their clients.** No matter how good a doctor may be, he or she must communicate effectively with you. Many times you, by expressing your concerns, will actually help diagnose your pet's problem.

For example, the historical information my patients provide is critical in allowing me to offer pets the best care possible, yet so many doctors rush through the history-taking part of the visit, and many owners often seem embarrassed to even mention any concerns. That's unfortunate because you're paying for an examination *and* a consultation. You have questions and concerns that need to be addressed. The most common complaint I hear from pet owners who come to me for a second opinion is that their previous veterinarians never listened to them or talked with them. How sad! There's no way doctors can make a correct diagnosis and prescribe the correct therapy without communicating with the client. The result is that the pet suffers by not receiving the care she needs.

There is no way I can offer good, holistic care for your pet unless I take the time you and your pet deserve and talk with you about all of your pet's needs. If you feel like going to the veterinarian is like being on a conveyor belt where you are rushed through the visit, it's time to find a doctor who truly has your pet's best interests at heart. I'm not surprised at the number of pets I see misdiagnosed and treated incorrectly when the owners tell me that the doctor didn't spend the time to do his job. In many cases a simple yet thorough physical examination was never even done by the previous doctor! Your pet deserves better than this.

Being a Good Owner

The other part of the health-care triangle that is important is obviously the owner, and that means *you*. Being a good, responsible pet owner is important if you want your dog to stay healthy and happy, to recover as quickly as possible if he does become ill or injured, and to minimize costs on pet care. Here are some qualities of a good, holistic-minded pet owner.

• **You are open to suggestions.** Just as a doctor rushing in and out of the examination room has a negative impact on your pet's health care, so does a client who is in a hurry to get somewhere. I see far too

Questions for Your Veterinarian

Once you locate someone you'd like to consider as a potential doctor for your pet, here are several questions to ask him or her:

- "How do you make a definitive diagnosis of disease in your patients?" This should be done by conventional laboratory testing and any other modalities (muscle testing, etc.) that may be helpful. A doctor who doesn't use conventional testing may miss certain disease processes simply by relying on unconventional testing.
- "What are your feelings about using drugs to treat disease?" The most holistic doctors recognize that drug therapy may be needed to help their patients. Ideally, their use should be limited until more natural therapies can help the pet heal, although some diseases are not curable and long-term use of conventional medications may be needed. Chronic use of conventional medications should be limited to the very rare pet that does not respond to any other therapy, and regular monitoring (every two to three months) of vital signs and laboratory tests is essential to allow early detection of side effects that can occur with drug therapy.
- "What type of diet should my pet eat?" The veterinarian should recommend the most natural prepared food with a limited amount of chemicals and animal and plant byproducts, or a natural homemade diet. Ideally, the type of food should match your pet's medical condition and state of health.
- "How do you treat chronic diseases?" The doctor should use supplements, herbs, homeopathy, acupuncture, or other complementary therapies to treat chronic diseases like arthritis. Holistic doctors rely on the rational use of conventional medications on a short-term, as-needed basis to help their patients, preferring more natural therapies for long-term healing needs.

many people who are in a rush when they come into the hospital with a pet requiring care. I can't possibly consult with you about everything your pet might need if you have only 10 to 15 minutes to visit since your child's school is letting out shortly and you need to pick her up. In order for you to get your money's worth, you must spend time during the visit so we can decide together what is best for your pet.

• **You communicate effectively with your veterinarian.** Yes, your veterinarian must talk with you, but you also must feel comfortable talking with him or her. While some doctors might have a "God" complex, many do not. No question or concern is stupid. It's your time, your money, and your pet. Make the visit worth your while.

• **Be realistic about what you can afford.** Most veterinarians will give owners an estimate of health-care costs. But first, you must let them know that cost is a concern to you. They will do what they can to not let cost be a factor in helping your pet get better. Finally, don't overlook the value of pet health insurance. For some owners, utilizing third-party payment often means the difference between treating their pets appropriately versus simply doing the least amount of care because that's all the owner can afford.

• **Allow the doctor to do what is necessary.** This point relates back to the cost issue. If the doctor needs to do several diagnostic tests, let him or her do them. It is usually less expensive to do the testing now rather than later if your pet continues to get worse. I am reminded of a recent new client who got very upset with me that her young kitten was still sneezing one week after her initial visit. I tried explaining to her that no matter how good a doctor I might be, I can never guarantee a cure. If her kitten had not improved after our initial diagnosis and therapy, I needed to re-examine the kitten and change our course of treatment. She refused, saying she did not want me "experimenting" with her kitten! The point I tried to stress to her was this: An owner who restricts my diagnostic efforts can't expect much from the treatment. Cooperate with your pet's doctor to maximize the chance of recovery and minimize the total cost to you.

WHAT ABOUT VACCINATIONS?

I've been talking a lot about the physical examination and the importance of taking a good, thorough history as the focus of Week 1

Personalized Pet Care

Several years ago, I came up with the idea of personalized pet care. I developed this concept more as a solution to the ever-increasing cost of pet health care, but then realized that it was perfect for my holistic approach. Occasionally, all doctors have to deal with clients who complain about how expensive it is to bring their pets in for health care. What if there was a way to minimize these complaints? That's when the idea of a more personalized approach came to me.

Here's how it works: After completing the physical examination and taking a thorough history, I formulate a diagnostic plan and treatment protocol. In most cases, there are several options for diagnosing and treating the pet. My belief is that the best plan, which I call "Plan A," should be offered first. Plan A is the one that does the most for the dog and has the greatest chance of diagnosing and successfully healing him. That's why I recommend it first. If a client finds this plan unsuitable at that time because of the cost (or for any other reason), then I work with the client to find the right plan for that client and pet on that particular day. This way, I can personalize a plan that fits every client's ability to pay.

By offering a diagnostic and treatment plan that fits a client's budget, I can personalize my recommendation to make the client happy. And no one can ever leave my office complaining that "it costs too much," because the client sets the limit on what she wants to spend that day.

It then occurred to me that this was a perfect approach to a holistic plan such as *8 Weeks to a Healthy Dog.* By recommending what I believe is best for the patient and then fine-tuning the plan

in our 8 Weeks to a Healthy Dog Program. You might be thinking, "And what about vaccinations for my dog?"

While many conventional doctors stress vaccinations as the most important (and sometimes only) part of the annual visit, my holistic colleagues and I take a very different approach. Certainly, a regular program of immunization is critical to prevent the common infectious diseases that in the past resulted in the unnecessary suffering and death of many dogs. Since they are inexpensive, vaccinations to the client's needs, this personalized approach is truly holistic.

What's really neat about this approach is that every treatment plan is different and unique. In many conventional practices, there is a cookie-cutter, one-treatment-fits-all approach. For example, let's say a client brings in her pet terrier for treatment of allergies. In the conventional approach, her dog—and every dog with allergies—will probably be treated with antihistamines or corticosteroids. By contrast, using the personalized, holistic approach, the way I treat her pet will be different from the way I treat the next dog with allergies. For example, maybe this client's dog will be treated with omega-3 fatty acids and antioxidants, plus bathing with an aloe vera–oatmeal shampoo every 48 hours. The next pet might be treated with herbs, homeopathics, and a medicated residual conditioner used two to three times daily.

By taking this personalized approach, I am able to look at both the pet's needs and the client's ability to follow my recommendations. Do you ever feel stupid when your doctor prescribes a treatment plan for your pet that you simply can't follow? Maybe you can't give your dog oral medication, or maybe you can't bathe your dog three times a week. Then why would the doctor not alter his recommendation based upon your needs? That's what personalized pet care is all about, and that's one of the great things about the 8 Weeks to a Healthy Dog Program—and about holistic pet care in general: Because holistic care is a more personalized, individualized type of health care than most pets receive, it makes it possible for you to work with your veterinarian to adapt any part of the 8-Week Program to suit what's best for you and your pet.

continue to be a cheap form of health insurance for many pets. And immunization with the rabies vaccine is essential in protecting the public from the threat of this disease.

Traditional, Conventional Care

In past years, most dogs died of infectious diseases such as rabies, distemper, and parvovirus. These pets never lived long enough to develop the chronic degenerative and immune problems we now see

ASK DR. SHAWN

Dear Dr. Shawn: "Is an annual rabies vaccination really necessary?"

A: In many states around the United States, it's required that owners get rabies vaccinations for their dogs and cats on an annual basis. Another requirement in many states is that we must use a three-year rabies vaccine. This means that every dog and cat vaccinated against rabies each year is given a vaccine that has been tested and labeled to provide immunity for at least three years. Holistic pet owners often ask me why I'm administering a vaccine annually, even though I know the vaccine provides protective immunity against rabies virus for three years. At this time, that is the law, and this is the way we must vaccinate against rabies. Because many of my clients do not want to vaccinate their pets if it is not really necessary, they face a dilemma. They can comply with the legal requirements and have me administer a vaccine to their pets that the pets do not need, or they can break the law and do what is best for their pets. Hopefully, the legal requirements will change and pet owners in the United States will not be forced to make a decision between complying with the law and doing what is medically in the best interests of their pets. I favor a three-year vaccine administered once every three years rather than a one-year vaccine administered annually, since it minimizes the number of injections each dog must receive. But either option is preferable to a three-year vaccine administered every year!

in our patients, such as cancer, kidney failure, and other organ failure. In the past, most dogs died after living only a few short months or years as a result of contracting these horrible, fatal infections.

Nowadays, because most dogs are properly immunized (or over-immunized!), it is rare for me to see a dog with hepatitis, distemper, or parvovirus. Many of my patients, because of the holistic health-care approach, live to be 12 to 20 years old. Instead of infectious diseases, I see older pets suffering from the following disorders:

• **Periodontal disease.** This is the most common infectious disease of dogs—it's estimated that over 99 percent of dogs have some degree of periodontal disease. This is easily treated with an annual dental scaling properly performed under anesthesia.

• **Cancer.** Many dogs have undiagnosed lumps and bumps that are often cancerous tumors. Unfortunately, many doctors look at and feel these lumps only when first mentioned by the pet owner, and they make a diagnosis of cyst or fatty tumor (both harmless conditions) simply by the look and feel of the lumps. I believe that, with very rare exceptions (the obvious wart or lump that has been present for years without a change in appearance), *all* lumps should be investigated by the veterinarian.

In most cases, aspiration cytology is all that's needed for diagnosis. Aspiration cytology is easy and inexpensive; it involves simply placing a tiny needle into the lump and aspirating cells or fluids with a syringe for microscopic analysis. This examination allows the doctor to tell if the lump is a simple cyst or fatty tumor (which usually does not require treatment) or something else that might need surgical removal and a more definitive diagnosis.

• **Heart disease.** A number of dogs have valvular heart disease, noticed as a heart murmur during their physical examination. I see too many pets who have been diagnosed with the heart murmur, but their previous doctors told the owners not to worry about the problem! All older dogs with heart murmurs should receive further evaluation—a heart murmur is always a sign of heart disease that can lead to heart failure.

• **Kidney disease.** A common killer in older dogs, kidney disease is easily diagnosed with an annual blood and/or urine test months to years before the dog actually becomes ill. With a holistic approach, early diagnosis and treatment will truly prevent an early, unexpected death.

• **Cognitive disorder.** Cognitive disorder, often referred to as "doggie Alzheimer's disease," is the most common neurological problem in older dogs. But early diagnosis and treatment can totally

On the Case with Dr. Shawn

DAISY

Just today I saw Daisy, an eight-year-old spayed female golden retriever, for evaluation of skin disease. During the course of the visit, Daisy's owner asked me to examine a small lump on her abdomen. The lump had been there for about six weeks and was not really bothering Daisy or her owner, but the owner was curious whether it was anything to worry about. The small mass resembled a typical fatty tumor, but as I always do, I aspirated the mass and examined the aspirate microscopically. This time, what appeared to be the common fatty tumor turned out in fact to be a cancerous mast cell tumor. Daisy is scheduled for surgery next week, and I believe our early diagnosis and treatment will cure her of what could have been a fatal cancer if left undiagnosed and treated. Daisy's observant owner, plus my aggressive approach to diagnosing the cause of what appeared to be a benign lump, have literally saved Daisy's life.

reverse the clinical signs in most patients. I treat dogs with this disorder with choline supplementation. (You can find an in-depth discussion of this disorder in my book the *Natural Health Bible for Dogs & Cats*.) I also believe that by administering choline to older dogs, we can actually prevent cognitive disorder in these patients. (For more about what choline is, what it does, and how to give it to your dog, see "Week 4: Choosing Nutritional Supplements for Your Dog," on page 95.)

A Better Alternative

As you can see, there is much more to health maintenance and disease prevention than just a few "yearly shots." Health care involves doing what's best for the entire pet, and each pet is an individual with unique needs; these needs differ from pet to pet, and may differ from month to month or year to year in the same dog.

As I've mentioned, vaccinations may not be necessary each year against every infectious disease your pet might encounter. Some dogs maintain protective antibody immunity longer than 12 months for some infectious diseases.

A better approach than the automatic recommendation to give every dog the same immunizations each year would be to run blood tests and determine vaccine titers. A titer tells us the antibody level of protection your dog has against a certain infectious disease. For example, if your dog has an antibody titer to parvovirus of 1:128, there is probably no reason to immunize him against parvovirus that year. If the titer is low, such as 1:2, he probably needs a current booster against parvovirus. This titer approach has worked well for me and many of my holistic colleagues, allowing us to administer fewer than half as many vaccines as in prior years.

If the annual vaccine titers are low, your veterinarian can administer vaccinations as needed. To minimize side effects from any immunizations that may need to be administered, many holistic doctors recommend using a homeopathic therapy such as thuja for several days following immunization. (Thuja is a prescription remedy; if your veterinarian practices homeopathy, you can ask him or her to discuss it with you and to prescribe it for your pet if needed.)

While vaccine antibody titers are easy to perform and they're inexpensive, they are not a perfect test. (Though, frankly, *no* laboratory test is perfect, since all have some degree of false positive and false negative results, and all tests require careful interpretation by a trained health-care provider.) Not all diseases produce a titer we can measure. For example, antibody levels have been shown to correlate with protection against distemper virus, parvovirus, adenovirus, and Lyme disease. Serum vaccine titers do not correlate with protection for kennel cough (caused by the bacterium *Bordetella bronchiseptica* and the parainfluenza virus) or coronavirus.

Antibody titers do give information about leptospirosis, although immunity against this disease following vaccination with inactivated leptospirosis organisms is generally believed to be short-lived (6 to

Side Effects from Vaccinations

Some pets develop side effects when they're vaccinated. These side effects can be divided into minor side effects (which rarely occur in most adult animals and are usually not serious) and major side effects (which are very rare but can be life-threatening). Major side effects such as anaphylactic shock have been proven to be a result of immunization in pets sensitized to the components in one or more vaccines. Some major side effects, such as cancer and immune diseases, are suspected to be related to vaccine use, but overwhelming scientific evidence of a true cause-and-effect relationship has not been demonstrated for all of these side effects. Both killed and modified live vaccines have been reported to cause vaccine reactions.

Most vaccine reactions occur following booster immunization with vaccines containing a number of antigens (5-way vaccines, 7-way vaccines, etc.). For this reason, if your veterinarian thinks your dog needs a vaccination, the least amount of vaccine should be used.

There's another possible side effect of vaccination: interference with the interpretation of various test results. Dogs vaccinated for Lyme disease will be positive on the screening test for this disorder, necessitating a follow-up test to differentiate between the vaccine and the actual presence of the disease.

While owners should not hesitate to have their pets immunized

12 months), and most dogs are immunized against only a few of the different strains of the leptospirosis bacterium.

Finally, there is no agreed-upon "correct" titer level for determining protective titers. Currently, doctors must use all of the conflicting information available and make an educated decision regarding what constitutes an "adequate protective" titer. In general, the following guidelines apply:

Distemper: Titers of less than 1:5, less than 1:20, or less than 1:96 have been recommended (most holistic veterinarians use the lower numbers, less than 1:5).

Parvovirus: Titers of less than 1:5 or less than 1:80 have been recommended (most holistic veterinarians use the lower numbers).

when needed, I recommend the holistic approach using vaccine titers to reduce the chance of side effects.

MINOR SIDE EFFECTS
Decreased appetite
Fever
Joint soreness
Lethargy
Stiffness

MAJOR SIDE EFFECTS
Atopic dermatitis (allergic dermatitis)
Autoimmune hemolytic anemia (decreased red blood cell count)
Autoimmune thrombocytopenia (decreased platelet count)
Bloating
Bone marrow suppression
Food allergy
Glomerulonephritis/renal amyloidosis (different types of immune kidney diseases)
Hypothyroidism
Immune system suppression
Kidney failure
Liver failure
Rheumatoid arthritis
Seizures
Systemic lupus erythematosus (lupus)

At your dog's exam, you can discuss these guidelines with your veterinarian (bring the book along to the veterinary hospital with you or just copy the page and bring it in). Your veterinarian can use the guidelines to determine which, if any, vaccines your dog may need at that time.

Even with the lack of complete agreement on the "correct" titer level, I share the belief of many of my holistic colleagues that the titer approach is far better for the pet than simply vaccinating every dog with every vaccine stored in the hospital refrigerator.

Keep in mind that, in the minds of many conventional doctors, this use of titers is a fairly radical approach to pet immunizations. But it really does make a lot of sense. This approach personalizes care for your pet and makes sure that she receives only the care she needs. It also places the main emphasis of the annual visit on the examination and laboratory testing, which is where it needs to be. It just doesn't make any sense to place the emphasis on immunizations when the main problems facing our pets are degenerative changes so commonly detected in our aging pet population.

While I've talked about using vaccine titers to determine if your dog needs any immunizations, this is not the only factor to consider. When I'm examining a dog, I also discuss the owner's needs and the pet's lifestyle to help determine which—if any—immunizations may be required. If, for example, the pet is a show dog that will be exposed to many other pets, the owner may desire (or the show may require) regular immunizations regardless of titer results. If the dog is an aggressive dog that could possibly bite someone, the owner may decide to have the rabies vaccine given to comply with the local legal requirements. Dogs that are frequently boarded may be given an intranasal bordetella immunization.

Finally, dogs with various diseases may not benefit from, and may be harmed as the result of, unnecessary immunization. In our practice, we never immunize pets that are ill. Pets with cancer never receive any more immunizations, as we do not want to harm their immune systems and cause a relapse of the cancer.

As you can see, in order to determine the need for immunization, the doctor must spend time with the client to truly personalize health-care recommendations for each and every pet. Make sure you discuss the use of vaccine titers with your veterinarian. If vaccines are needed based on your pet's lifestyle and titer results, have your pet immunized as needed at the start of our program.

WRAPPING UP

As we end the first week of our 8 Weeks to a Healthy Dog Program, I hope you've scheduled and had your veterinarian give your dog a

On the Case with Dr. Shawn

CODY

Cody is a four-year-old terrier with allergic skin disease (atopic der-matitis). Because over-immunization might exacerbate his allergies, his owners decided to check his vaccine titers annually to determine which, if any, vaccinations might be needed. His titers were high for most diseases; however, despite annual vaccination in the past, his parvovirus titer was low at 1:4. Therefore, this year he received im-munization against this horrible disease, but he did not receive any other immunizations, which I felt were not needed. Next year, we'll repeat his titers and see if his immunization this year is still protec-tive after 12 months.

thorough physical examination and the necessary laboratory testing. Hopefully, no major problems were discovered. (If the examination and lab testing did show any problems, we'll address these in "Week 5: Treating Diseases Naturally" on page 120.) In the next chapter, we'll talk about a common concern expressed by many pet owners: preventing and treating internal and external parasites.

4

WEEK 2:
Treating Parasites

Fleas. Ticks. Heartworms. No one really likes to think about creepy, crawly bugs, but let's face it, they outnumber us here on earth, so they're pretty unavoidable. In this chapter, I'll talk about the most common parasites, discuss conventional treatments for them, and offer some effective approaches to rid your dog of them naturally.

Parasites cause many illnesses in dogs, such as anemia, itchy skin, and mange. My educated guess is that almost 100 percent of puppies have internal parasites and that 50 to 75 percent of adult dogs are exposed to parasites at some point in their lives. While the harmful effects of these parasites are not always apparent, we know that they can cause debilitating diseases and weaken your dog. Therefore, for your dog to have a healthy life, it's important to make sure she's not harboring internal or external parasites.

Just in case you need a more compelling reason than that to read on, here you go. After they've taken hold on your dog, parasites can move on to *you*. Some parasites, such as roundworms and hookworms, can infect people, too. Other parasites, such as ticks, transmit diseases like Rocky Mountain spotted fever to people. It's very important—you must keep your dog parasite-free to protect your health as well.

Parasites can be broken down into two groups: external and internal parasites. Let's look at them (ugh! I know, but bear with me) a little more closely.

EXTERNAL PARASITES

The one good thing, if you can call it that, about external parasites is you can see them. Most external parasites live on a dog's skin and are usually perfectly visible. The one exception is mites, which are microscopic. Common external parasites include fleas, lice, mites, and ticks.

Fleas and Ticks

Because similar preventive steps and treatments work for both fleas and ticks, we'll cover them together here. First, the fleas. Fleas are probably the most familiar parasite. They hitch rides on dogs—and pretty much any other warm-blooded animal—and suck their blood. Flea bites cause a dog's skin to itch like crazy. If a dog has enough fleas, they actually deplete the dog's blood volume, forcing the bone marrow to work harder to maintain an adequate supply of red blood cells, white blood cells, and platelets. This can be very dangerous. It can cause severe and occasionally fatal anemia in puppies and smaller dogs such as Chihuahuas, Malteses, and the smaller terriers.

If your dog has fleas, you're likely to see the pests' small, flat bodies crawling or jumping on your dog. They're often found on a dog's hindquarters or behind his ears, places where the dog can't easily scratch them off. Fleas can jump 150 times their own length, as high as 4 feet. You also may spot flea dirt on or around your dog. These tiny, black specks resemble coffee grounds.

Besides the harm they do to a dog all by themselves, fleas also carry tapeworms and can transmit them to your dog. Tapeworms are a type of internal parasite that infect a dog's intestines and compete with the dog's body for vital nutrients. Sometimes a dog's owner, or veterinarian, will see tapeworm segments in the dog's feces and realize that the dog has a flea problem. (Hold that thought; we'll talk more about tapeworms on page 64.)

Ticks have been the parasite in the news lately. Ticks are small,

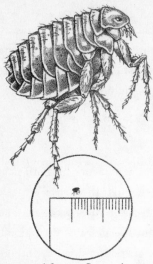

Here's a life-size flea and one that's magnified to show detail.

black, eight-legged insects that slightly resemble flattened spiders. They attach themselves to a host's body, sucking blood. If a dog has enough ticks, they can actually deplete the dog's blood volume. But even more dangerous are the diseases they transmit.

Ticks transmit potentially fatal infections, including Rocky Mountain spotted fever, ehrlichiosis, and Lyme disease, that can affect dogs and people who are bitten by ticks.

Warning signs that your dog may have been bitten by a tick include cough, fever, lameness, and loss of appetite. You're most likely to see a tick on your dog's skin or feel it when you pet your dog.

If you find a tick on your dog, carefully remove it with a tweezers. Grasp the tick near your dog's skin where the tick's head is attached. Gently but firmly pull on the tick's body until the head releases from the dog. (Applying a drop of rubbing alcohol or cooking oil to the tick before removal may help loosen the tick.) Save the tick in a jar filled with rubbing alcohol to kill the tick, and close the jar with a lid in case your veterinarian needs to determine what kind of tick it is or wants to run tests to see if it is carrying disease. Don't handle ticks with your hands because they can carry diseases—use the tweezers to hold it or wear latex gloves.

About one to two months after you remove a tick from your dog, ask your veterinarian to run blood tests to determine if your dog is infected with any tick-related diseases. Infected dogs can be easily treated with antibiotics and immune-boosting supplements when the infection is detected early, before severe symptoms occur. Re-

On the Case with Dr. Shawn
CASEY

Casey is a small, black-haired, male mixed-breed dog. During his an-nual visit, I noticed that small, black flecks had fallen off of Casey and onto our white examining table. These black flecks, called "flea dirt," are flea fecal material. I pointed out these droppings to the owner, who really didn't believe they could be flea material. She in-sisted that her dog "didn't have fleas."

I applied a small drop of water to a few of the droppings, which then turned red. This happens because the flea droppings are dried blood. So, when they're rehydrated with a drop of water, the black turns red. That convinced her! (You can use this trick at home if you see black specks, too.)

Since I was able to prove to his owner that Casey did in fact have fleas, even though we did not see fleas on him that day, we placed Casey on a flea preventive and treatment program like the one I rec-ommend below.

peated tests will determine if the drug and supplement therapy has cleared the infection.

What to do: Despite your best efforts, fleas and ticks may still take up residence on your dog. Don't be too discouraged—these little buggers are hard to beat. You're in good company, and the market has responded with lots of products to get rid of them.

In the past, conventional therapies for fleas and ticks included collars, dips, powders, and sprays. These products were potentially toxic to the dog, and they were also toxic to the owner. Not surpris-ingly, most holistic veterinarians—including me!—stay away from these products.

Over the last 10 years, pharmaceutical companies have devel-oped products that are less toxic than these older therapies. They're easier to give to your dog, too. Here are some common products:

Once-a-month tablets: You give these tablets to your dog once a month. In his system, they sterilize adult fleas, making them unable

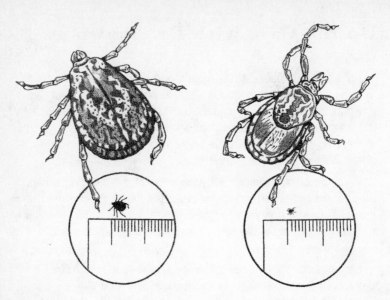

Here's a life-size dog tick and the much smaller deer tick, and one of each magnified to show detail.

to reproduce in your house and yard. This product can also be used to prevent fleas. They're sold at pet stores and veterinary hospitals.

Once-a-month topical treatments: Also available at veterinary hospitals, these solutions are applied to your dog's skin. Although they're designed to be used once a month, some products are so effective against fleas they need only be administered every two to three months. (Ask your veterinarian how often he or she recommends applying a specific product.) These products kill adult fleas. Combining the topical products with the oral tablet gives good comprehensive flea control.

I believe these products can be used most holistically when given during the periods of the year when fleas and ticks are likely to cause problems, such as in the summer. I advise owners not to use them the rest of the year. This decreases cost to the owner and prevents the needless year-round administration of chemicals that aren't necessary when external parasites are not likely to infest pets.

Lice

Lice occur less commonly in dogs than fleas or ticks. Lice are small, flattened insects. There are two types, biting lice and blood-sucking lice. Both types cause red, scabby areas on a dog's skin that are very tender and can itch terribly. Lice are spread through direct contact between dogs or by shared grooming tools. Signs of lice include scratching and a smelly coat. Rarely, people can get lice from their pets.

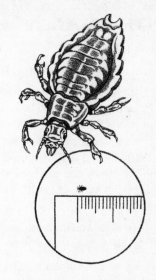

Here's a life-size louse and one magnified to show detail.

What to do: The most common conventional treatment for lice is insecticide shampoo. You'll find it at veterinary hospitals. While the label may not specifically say it's for lice, any shampoo made for fleas will work.

Mites

Mites are commonly diagnosed in both puppies and older dogs. Unlike fleas, lice, and ticks, mites are so tiny that they are not visible to the naked eye. You're likely to know that your dog has mites only if he comes down with the disease that they cause. Mites cause a disease called mange that affects dogs' skin. There are two types of skin mange, demodectic mange and sarcoptic mange, which are caused by two different types of mites.

Demodectic mange

Demodectic mange is the first and most common type of mange. It's caused by a type of mite called demodectic mites. All puppies actually get demodectic mites from their mothers within hours of being born. Because of this, all puppies and dogs have these mites living

On the Case with Dr. Shawn

SALLY

This is a sad, cautionary tale.

Sally is a four-year-old spayed female Pekingese. Her owner noticed her white-haired body was covered with fleas and ticks. Instead
of taking Sally to a veterinarian to determine the safest, most effective treatment, Sally's owner decided to treat the parasites himself.
He happened to have an old bottle of "cattle tick dip" that someone
in the family had used previously on the family farm. He figured that
if the dip killed cattle ticks, it could certainly kill the fleas and ticks
on Sally.

The dip worked quite well in killing the parasites covering Sally's
body. However, it also nearly killed Sally.

I saw Sally on an emergency basis over the Fourth of July weekend. She was showing signs of severe organophosphate poisoning, as
well as severe anemia from the excessive infestation of fleas and
ticks. (She probably also had a tick-borne disease such as ehrlichiosis, but we were not able to test for that on an emergency
basis.) This poor dog was literally struggling for life.

We immediately bathed the poisoned dog to remove any residual
"cattle dip." Then we placed her in an oxygenated cage to help her
anemic blood transport oxygen throughout her body and gave her a
massive blood transfusion. Twenty-four hours and $450 later, Sally
was discharged with instructions to take her back to her regular veterinarian for continued treatment.

I never found out if Sally survived her flea and tick treatment. Her
prognosis was not good based upon the severity of her reaction to the
improper treatment.

While I still occasionally see this type of severe reaction when
owners incorrectly use flea and tick products, thankfully our prescription products are much safer today. There is never a reason for
a dog to become poisoned by any commercial flea or tick insecticidal
products. And for owners who choose a more natural approach to parasite control, administered under veterinary supervision, side effects
are also very rare.

DR. SHAWN'S TRICKS OF THE TRADE

Owners often ask me if they must use products sold by their veterinarians, or if they can use insecticide products found at local pet or grocery stores. While some of these over-the-counter products can be useful, others are potentially more toxic—and messy—than veterinary-prescribed insecticides. Work with your veterinarian to determine the best pest control for your dog.

normally within their hair follicles. Most of the time, these mites live out their lives on dogs' skin and do not cause problems.

However, if a dog has a suppressed immune system, or in puppies whose immune systems aren't fully developed, the mites can run amok. The mites reproduce and excessively colonize the skin, and the dog develops demodectic mange. This type of mange causes hair loss and sometimes scaling of the skin.

The only way to prevent demodectic mange is to keep your puppy as healthy as possible, and to avoid breeding dogs that have developed demodectic mange. This type of mange is rare in older dogs because they normally have more mature, "competent" immune systems. When it does occur in older dogs, it is important to look for any problems that may have occurred to affect the pet's immune system, such as cancer or steroid therapy.

To diagnose demodectic mange, veterinarians do a simple laboratory test called a skin scraping. They scrape debris from the skin and examine it microscopically for the presence of the mange mites. We'll talk about how veterinarians treat it on page 56.

Sarcoptic mange

The second type of mange is called sarcoptic mange, which is caused by a different type of mite. It can occur in puppies or older dogs and is not associated with suppression of the immune system. Unlike demodectic mange, sarcoptic mange is very itchy to the pet. Dogs can catch it from each other and even give it to people via close contact with the infected dog and anything that has contacted the infected dog, such as bedding and brushes.

Veterinarians diagnose this type of mange also by looking at skin scrapings under a microscope, but the sarcoptic mites are much harder to detect than demodectic mites. In fact, half of all dogs infected with sarcoptic mange may not show mites even on multiple skin scrapings.

Because of this, veterinarians often treat dogs for sarcoptic mange based only on the symptoms—itchy, scaly skin—even if the mites are not detected microscopically.

What to do: The conventional treatment for mites that cause mange is potent dips. These dips must be properly prepared, and the person applying the dip should wear protective clothing to minimize contact with the dip. Because these dips are so toxic if not properly mixed, I usually recommend having them done at your dog's veterinarian's office. If your dog must have a dip, monitor her carefully for about eight hours following the dip for these rare side effects: bloating, diarrhea, lethargy, tremors, and vomiting.

While I prefer not to dip pets except those with severe mange, in most cases the dips are safe and quite effective. To minimize the number of dips needed to successfully treat mange, I always like to combine the dipping with some of the supplements discussed on page 58 to help the pet heal as quickly as possible.

Ear mites

You may have heard of a different type of mite that affects dogs—the ear mite. These tiny bugs usually take up residence in a dog's ear canal. Dogs with ear mites scratch around their ears or shake their heads frantically. If the mites really take hold, the ear canal can bleed. You may see dried blood inside your dog's ear. It looks like coffee grounds.

Veterinarians diagnose ear mites by gathering some of the debris from the dog's ears and looking at it under a microscope. Because ear itching can also be caused by a bacterial or yeast infection in a dog's ears, it's important that the veterinarian do this test so that the proper treatment can begin.

If a dog has ear mites, the veterinarian will flush her ears to get rid of the mites and then treat her with oral or injectable medicine called ivermectin or topical insecticides such as Otomax or Tresaderm. Or your veterinarian might use an herbal ear wash containing various oils such as neem, tea tree oil, or peppermint oil. Your dog's veterinarian will also treat your dog's whole body with topical conventional or natural flea products if only ear drops are prescribed rather than oral or injectable ivermectin.

Preventing External Parasites

After reading all of that, you may be thinking, okay that all sounds so unpleasant, how can I just prevent my dog from getting fleas, lice, mites, and ticks to start with? In general, you're already on the right track by putting your dog on my 8-Week Program. Most holistic doctors agree that healthy dogs that eat the best, most natural diets are less likely to be bothered by parasites. And, if they do become infested with parasites, these dogs are less likely to suffer ill effects. Here are some of my favorite ways to prevent external parasites:

Minimize exposure. Before they can infest your dog, external parasites such as fleas, lice, mites, and ticks must establish themselves in your pet's environment. So, if you minimize your dog's exposure to them, there is little chance your pet will ever have to deal with external parasites.

For example, when you take your dog for a walk, don't be so quick to let him run in grassy or wooded areas where parasites like ticks live. Instead, stick to sidewalks and other concrete areas that are free of parasites. Since some parasites must literally hop from animal to animal, keeping your dog away from other dogs can minimize his exposure, too.

Brush them off. If you do allow your dog to romp through the

fields, carefully inspect his skin and coat before bringing him back in
your yard and house. Brush off any parasites you see. Flea combs,
sold at pet stores, work great for this. Use them to remove any bugs
you see on the coat and skin. Put the fleas or ticks into a jar of alcohol for disposal.

Get them out of your yard. Sometimes, despite your best efforts,
parasites take up residence in your yard. The neighbor's dog or cat
or local wildlife such as squirrels may deposit flea eggs in the grass,
which hatch into hungry adult fleas. Treating the yard with natural
insecticides such as diatomaceous earth or beneficial nematodes,
which are microscopic worms that actually eat the flea larvae, will
kill the fleas and prevent them from infesting your dog.

Try supplements. Adding garlic or brewer's yeast to your dog's
food may also help prevent parasites. See pages 59 and 60 for
amounts.

Natural Therapies for External Parasites

Although conventional medicine offers the many effective, safe
treatments for fleas, ticks, lice, and mites that I described, holistic pet
owners usually prefer more natural therapies. While these natural
therapies are usually less toxic than their conventional counterparts,
any product can be toxic if it's used incorrectly. Always follow
package directions.

In some cases, the most holistic approach involves a combination
of the newer chemical insecticides plus one or more natural therapies. For instance, you might use a chemical dip to quickly kill the
parasites and then rely on the natural products to keep the bugs at
bay in the future. Because a parasite infection is a serious problem
that can lead to disease, it's important to work with your veterinarian
to choose the best therapy for your dog.

The only disadvantage of these natural external parasite remedies is that they often require frequent application, which makes
them inconvenient for owners with a large number of dogs or little

time to properly administer them. Here are my top natural therapies for fleas, lice, and ticks:

Carpet and yard treatments. If you see one flea on your dog, there are probably hundreds more lurking in your furniture, carpets, and yard. That's why it's critical to treat your environment, not just your dog, for fleas. Treat your carpets with a borate product specifically manufactured for flea control, such as Flea Stoppers. Vacuum and steam-clean your carpets regularly to remove larvae and cocoons.

Natural diatomaceous earth (not the kind used in swimming pools) is also effective indoors and outdoors. You'll find it for sale in garden supply catalogs like Gardens Alive. Sprinkle it liberally around your yard. It can also help control fleas, ticks, and lice on your dog. Apply the powder lightly to your pet's coat and massage it in.

Beneficial nematodes, which are microscopic worms that actually eat the flea larvae, are also very helpful. Interestingly, nematodes are the only treatment that kill the cocoon stage of the flea life cycle. Even chemical yard sprays do not do this. You can buy beneficial nematodes at garden centers, from gardening supply catalogs, and on gardening Web sites.

Flea powders, shampoos, and sprays. Look for powders, shampoos, and sprays containing citrus extract, such as d-limonene. Or choose products containing natural pyrethrum, the flowers of the chrysanthemum plant. It is the least toxic type of insecticide. While these products are usually safer than similar products containing other classes of chemicals, they still can be toxic if used incorrectly, so read the label and exercise care.

You can make your own citrus pour-on solution by slicing an unpeeled orange, lemon, or lime and adding it to 1 quart of boiling water. After the mixture cools, apply it to your dog's skin as needed.

Garlic. Sprinkle garlic powder lightly on each of your dog's meals. Or feed him approximately 1 clove, either raw or cooked with a little olive oil, per 10 pounds of body weight, each day. Many dog owners find this reduces external parasites.

DR. SHAWN SAYS

Many dog owners swear that brewer's yeast keeps their dogs free of external parasites, but studies show it is ineffective. Brewer's yeast contains B vitamins that are excreted through eccrine sweat glands. The strong odor and taste repel fleas. The only problem is that a dog does not have this type of sweat glands over most of his body as we do, which is why dogs don't sweat. Their only sweat glands are on their foot pads and noses, but fleas don't normally infest these areas. So, although some owners swear by brewer's yeast, and it certainly won't hurt your dog, it may not be adequate as the sole product to prevent and treat flea problems.

If you want to try it, add 1 teaspoon to 2 tablespoons of brewer's yeast to each of your dog's meals.

Garlic contains nutrients and sulfur compounds, such as allicin and alliin, that have been shown to have medical qualities. Raw garlic kills microorganisms, including fungi, bacteria, viruses, and protozoa, on contact. That's why I think that adding garlic oil to a topical dip for fleas would work better than feeding it to a dog.

But some owners swear by garlic. While all of the conventional research I have read contradicts these owners' observations, I have no problem recommending it. If it works, it's quite simple and non-toxic. If it doesn't help, you are free to choose another remedy. As long as you don't add more garlic than I recommend or add onions to the food, which can cause anemia, this regimen is not harmful and may help control external parasites.

Topical treatments. While these herbs won't get rid of parasites, they can soothe your dog's itchy skin. Apply herbal rinses such as aloe vera, calendula, lavender, peppermint, and yarrow. This is especially helpful for pets with flea allergic dermatitis.

Compared with fleas, ticks, and lice, it is much more difficult to get rid of mite infestations with natural therapies. I usually find I have to dip dogs unless their disease is localized to one or two spots.

For localized disease, diluted garlic oil or tea tree oil may help. Applying the herb mullein topically may also prove useful. Even when I have to dip pets with demodectic mange, giving dogs supplements such as echinacea, arabinogalactans (the active ingredient in the larch plant), and homeopathic sulfur to boost the immune system reduces the number of dips needed to treat the mange. You can purchase these supplements at your veterinarian's office.

Ear mites are easier to treat with natural therapies and often respond to four weeks of therapy with peppermint oil mixed with tea tree oil. Place a few drops of the mixture into your dog's ears each day. Because mites can live outside of the ears, it is wise to treat the pet's body as well. Any of the topical flea treatments will usually work.

INTERNAL PARASITES

While the presence of external parasites such as fleas and ticks is usually obvious, your dog could have internal parasites and you may never see them. Two clues are diarrhea and itchy skin. Many owners are not even aware that their pets have an internal parasite problem. That's why I recommend taking your dog to the veterinarian for a parasite evaluation each year.

The most common internal parasites are various "worms," such as heartworms, hookworms, roundworms, tapeworms, and whipworms. Other internal parasites are protozoal infections, including giardial infections and coccidial infections. Any of these parasites may cause diarrhea, gastrointestinal pain, gas, weight loss, or failure

DR. SHAWN SAYS

Here's a very important caution. Some natural therapies that have traditionally been used for parasites are extremely dangerous to dogs. They're actually *more* dangerous than the newer chemical insecticides. Do not give your dog the herbs black walnut or wormwood or use pennyroyal oil on his skin. They can be very toxic.

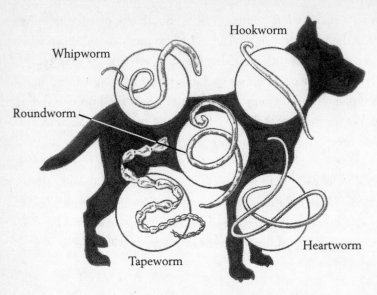

Here are five common internal parasites ("worms"), magnified to show detail.

to thrive. Hookworms may also cause anemia because these parasites are bloodsuckers. Symptoms of internal parasites are more severe in younger and smaller dogs.

Since they're not external, your veterinarian needs to diagnose internal parasites. Most commonly, veterinarians check for internal parasites by looking for parasite eggs in a dog's feces under a microscope. I recommend that this be done at least annually, and preferably every three to six months. Because the eggs of internal parasites may not be shed in the feces every day, the more often the tests are performed, the greater the chance of a correct diagnosis.

I recommend that if your dog has not had a microscopic fecal examination within the last three to six months, you should have your dog's feces checked at the start of the 8-Week Program.

If your pet is infected with parasites, have him treated right away. Then, begin a regular preventive program, including the monthly heartworm preventive medication that we'll talk about more on the next page.

Some owners, especially those in high-parasite environments, may choose to give their dogs a "deworming" medication every three to six months to help prevent parasite infections. This is commonly done with horses. While rarely needed in dogs, this practice is safe and is often needed in pets that have frequent exposure to parasites. Since parasite problems are usually most severe in animals eating inadequate diets or those in poor health, a good diet is in order (see "Week 3: Choosing the Best Diet for Your Dog" on page 73), as is a state of overall good health (see "Week 1: The Veterinary Visit" on page 29).

Here's some more detailed information on the two most common internal parasites, heartworms and tapeworms, and what conventional and natural medicine offer to prevent and treat them.

Heartworms

Heartworms are internal parasites that infect the heart, lungs, and associated blood vessels. These internal parasites are carried by mosquitos. When a mosquito bites your dog, it injects microscopic heartworm larvae into your dog's body. Heartworms can cause severe debilitation and even sudden death in dogs.

An ounce of prevention

It's easy to prevent heartworms by giving your dog a monthly medication, such as ivermectin or milbemycin. Prevention is much better than treatment, which is expensive. You've probably seen commercials or heard about the once-a-month heartworm pills. These drugs very effectively prevent heartworms. Most dogs really enjoy these tasty heartworm "treats."

As a great bonus, many heartworm prevention pills contain additional medication to help prevent intestinal parasites. This is also safe and can help keep your dog worm-free.

Treating heartworms

If your veterinarian finds that your dog already has heartworms, this is cause for concern. Treating heartworms is a more serious and complicated matter. Treatment also used to be very dangerous. The old way of treating heartworms was to inject arsenic into a dog, which could be quite toxic. A newer drug called Immiticide has made treatment much safer. This drug is injected into your dog's muscles, which makes it easy to administer and decreases the chance of side effects. I have not experienced any serious problems with the use of Immiticide in my practice.

Another conventional treatment for heartworms is to give your dog the monthly heartworm prevention medicine. (If your dog gets heartworms, you'll certainly wish you had given it to him *before* to prevent this terrible condition!) Studies show that using these medicines, which contain ivermectin, for 6 to 12 months can kill some of the adult parasites.

Because heartworm treatments are so powerful, I carefully evaluate each of my heartworm patients to be sure other problems do not exist that might complicate therapy. By screening for other problems—such as liver, kidney, or heart disease—with x-rays, electrocardiograms, and blood and urine tests, I can determine which pets can be safely treated. I always like to combine the Immiticide therapy with several natural remedies to help reduce toxicity and side effects from the Immiticide. We'll talk about them later on page 70.

Tapeworms

You'll remember that I mentioned tapeworms on page 49, while talking about fleas. Fleas, in addition to their many other annoying traits, transmit tapeworms to dogs. How they do this is a very interesting, and pretty gross, process.

Tapeworms live in dogs' intestines, living off the dogs' nutrients. When a dog eats flea eggs, some of them end up in the tapeworms. Tapeworms are long, flat worms composed of many smaller segments that resemble grains of white rice. Some of these segments, which contain tapeworm eggs, break off and appear in dogs' feces.

ASK DR. SHAWN

Dear Dr. Shawn: "Is it really safe to give my dog heartworm prevention medicine each and every month for life?"

A: Many of my holistic dog owners ask this. After all, keeping your dog on chronic medication does not seem like a particularly holistic thing to do.

In this case, though, it's the smart way to go. I have two big reasons for that. First, preventing disease is certainly more holistic than having to treat one. Simply stated, this medicine will keep your dog from getting a potentially deadly disease.

Second, it is important for pet owners to know that the monthly medications do not stay in the dog's body the entire month. I'll explain why. Let's say that you give your dog her monthly heartworm preventive medication today. The medicine immediately kills any microfilariae (microscopic heartworm larvae injected by the mosquito when it feeds on your dog) in the dog's body. However, the half-life of the medicine is quite short. Within the week following administration of the medication, it's out of your dog's system. If your dog is infected with more microfilariae next week, since there is no longer any active heartworm preventive in her body, these microfilariae will not be killed and will begin growing. When you give your dog the heartworm preventive next month, however, the medicine will kill any microfilariae that are present in your dog's body.

So while the medicine does not last the entire month, based upon how it works and the heartworm life cycle, monthly administration is all that your dog needs.

Some owners ask about the new six-month injectable preventive medication, which is called ProHeart 6. While it seems to work, I prefer not to use it. This drug stays in the dog's body the entire six months. I believe a more holistic approach is to use the monthly preventive oral medication that stays in the pet's body for only a few days.

Fleas feed on these segments and ingest the tapeworm eggs contained in the tapeworm segments. The eggs hatch into baby tapeworms inside the flea. The life cycle of the tapeworm is completed when the dog eats the flea crawling on its body, causing the baby tapeworm located in the flea's body to come out of the flea and attach to the dog's intestine, where it will obtain nutrients, grow, and continue its reproductive cycle.

An ounce of prevention

The only way to prevent tapeworms is to use excellent flea control. Beef up your flea-prevention measures, as we discussed on page 57.

Treating tapeworms

Surely you're hoping by now that your dog never has to deal with tapeworms! In past years, the deworming medications were often worse than the disease. Dogs experienced violent abdominal contractions as they forcefully vomited dying worms or expelled them from their large intestines, spewing large volumes of feces containing the parasites for several days.

Thankfully, the newer chemical deworming drugs we have are very safe and effective. The conventional treatment for tapeworms includes the drug praziquantel. Dogs that are dewormed with our current parasitic treatments almost never show any of these side effects. After your dog is treated, your veterinarian must do a follow-up microscopic fecal examination to make sure that the tapeworms are gone.

Preventing Internal Parasites

As is the case with preventing external parasites, most holistic doctors agree that healthy dogs that eat the best, most natural diets are less likely to be bothered by parasites. If they do become infested with parasites, these dogs are less likely to suffer ill effects.

As a nice bonus of age, your dog is less likely to get some internal parasites as he gets older. For example, while puppies often have roundworm infections, older dogs rarely have this problem because their mature immune systems usually prevent ingested worm eggs from developing into adult parasites. Here are some ways to prevent internal parasites:

Minimize exposure. As is the case with external parasites, there are things you can do to keep your dog away from internal parasites so she won't become infected by them. For example, because tapeworms are carried by fleas, practicing good flea control will keep

---

ASK DR. SHAWN

Dear Dr. Shawn: "I'm not sure what to do. I took my dog to the veterinarian, and he treated the dog for worms, but my dog still has them!"

A: I often see clients whose pets have been dewormed by other veterinarians. These owners are concerned because the dogs are still infected with the parasites despite what appeared to be the proper therapy.

In most cases, I have been able to determine that one of two situations has occurred. First, the root cause of the problem was not addressed. This is most often the case with dogs infected with tapeworms. Since tapeworms are carried by fleas, unless all pets in the environment—and the environment itself—are treated for fleas, the pet will continue to become infected with tapeworms. Because our modern deworming medications are so effective against intestinal parasites, the persistence of tapeworm infections in pets almost always indicates lack of proper flea control.

The second situation occurs when the proper treatment was prescribed but the number of dewormings or intervals between treatments were incorrect. This is usually the case with dogs infected with the intestinal parasites called whipworms. Whipworms are an infrequent cause of bowel problems such as diarrhea, gas, and cramping, and they are very difficult to diagnose. Once diagnosed, however, they are easily treated if the proper number of treatments and treatment intervals is prescribed.

To properly eradicate whipworms, dogs must undergo at least three treatments, which are usually done at home, using a drug called fenbendazole. The first therapy is administered when the dog is diagnosed. Treatment is repeated again in three weeks, and the final treatment is given again three months from the first treatment. (The problem is most doctors do not remember this third therapy.) So if your pet has persistent parasite infections, the cause can usually be discovered and the proper treatment instituted to solve the problem.

On the Case with Dr. Shawn

NICKY

Nicky is a spayed female Sheltie. Her owner brought her in because she saw "worms" in Nicky's feces that morning. I asked her to bring in the fecal sample containing the "worms."

Nicky's feces did in fact contain worms, or actually pieces of worms. It turned out that Nicky had tapeworms. In the feces, her owner was seeing pieces of the worms. These segments, called proglottid segments, actually contain the worm eggs. And again in this case, I knew that Nicky had fleas, because dogs become infected with tapeworms by eating fleas. Even though we did not detect fleas on Nicky, I knew by seeing the tapeworm segments that she had recently been infected with fleas.

So, in addition to treating Nicky for tapeworms, we also started her on a flea-control program, including herbal dips and powders. With these two treatments, Nicky should be bug-free in a matter of weeks.

tapeworms away from your dog. Other intestinal parasites are transmitted by the fecal-oral route. This means that your pet will get them if she ingests infected feces. Avoiding common areas where pets eliminate will help reduce the chance of your dog contacting contaminated feces.

Try diatomaceous earth. Some holistic folks advocate feeding food-grade—not pool-grade—diatomaceous earth as prevention (and treatment) for several worm infestations. (You can find food-grade diatomaceous earth, also called DE, at pet stores and garden centers.) Give your dog diatomaceous earth with his food each day— 1 teaspoon of diatomaceous earth for each 25 pounds of body weight. It's odorless and tasteless, so your dog should never notice the difference!

Give monthly medications. Using the monthly heartworm preventive medications is almost guaranteed to prevent your dog from ever contracting this potentially fatal problem. As one great bonus, this monthly treatment usually also contains additional medication to decrease the chance of intestinal parasites, such as tapeworms.

Instead of using this proven monthly medication, some doctors substitute a homeopathic heartworm nosode to prevent heartworms. I have not seen proof that it works, so I do not recommend its use. If you elect to use the nosode as a preventive in place of the safe, proven conventional preventive medications available, I recommend a heartworm antigen test at least every six months to allow early diagnosis and treatment if your dog gets heartworms.

Natural Therapies for Internal Parasites

Despite our best holistic preventive efforts, some pets will get internal parasites and require treatment. If that happens to your dog, consider the following natural therapies:

Pumpkin seeds. Grind a handful of fresh, raw pumpkin seeds into your pet's meal. Give your dog ¼ to 1 teaspoon per 10 to 20 pounds of body weight at each meal for several weeks.

Wheat germ oil. Give your dog ¼ to 1 teaspoon of wheat germ oil per 10 to 20 pounds of body weight at each meal for several weeks. You can buy it at health food stores.

Diatomaceous earth. Natural—food-grade, not pool-grade— diatomaceous earth may effectively treat, as well as prevent, intestinal parasites. Administered directly in the food at approximately 1 teaspoon per 25 pounds of body weight, natural diatomaceous earth is safe and tasteless.

Garlic. The herb garlic contains a number of nutrients and sulfur compounds that have been shown to have medicinal qualities, especially allicin and alliin. Raw garlic kills microorganisms on contact, including fungi, bacteria, viruses, and protozoa. Garlic is recommended for dogs with tapeworms. It has been proven effective in treating people with roundworms and hookworms, and it is often recommended for pets with these parasites, as well.

In general, I recommend mixing 1 clove (not the entire head) of garlic for each 10 to 20 pounds of body weight right in with your dog's food each day. You can give the garlic to your dog raw, or sauté it with olive oil before putting it the food. Don't use more than recommended, though. Too much can cause anemia.

Homeopathics. Homeopathic remedies suggested for intestinal parasites include cina and filix mas. Talk with your veterinarian about dosages.

Plant enzymes. These enzymes, such as Prozyme, can be added to your dog's food or given as a nutritional supplement. Simply sprinkle them on your dog's food or follow the directions on the label. These enzymes won't get rid of parasites, but because they contain cellulase, they aid in digestion and help your dog absorb nutrients, so the worms don't get them all!

Herbs. Protozoal infections such as giardiasis and cocciodiosis may respond to therapy with the herbs Oregon grape and goldenseal, although conventional medications are usually necessary to treat these infections.

Supplements. While there are no natural alternative therapies to get rid of heartworms, some supplements can support a dog while he goes through conventional heartworm treatment. I usually use herbs such as milk thistle to strengthen the liver and aid in detoxification of the conventional medications used to treat heartworm infection. Supplements to strengthen the heart, such as coenzyme Q10 and the herb hawthorn, may also be beneficial. Antioxidants are always helpful as part of the therapy for any disease which may cause oxidative damage to tissues as a result of injury to cells.

While these various natural treatments are widely used with variable success, they have not been thoroughly investigated and proven at this time. However, I see no harm in trying them (with veterinary supervision). You can always try a conventional dewormer if the natural therapies fail to treat the infection. Simply have your veterinarian repeat a microscopic fecal analysis after you've begun treatment to see if the therapy is working, just as

Doggie Dosages

Even though lots of holistic veterinarians prescribe herbs for dogs, there aren't many companies that make herbal products specifically for dogs. See "Sources for Natural Foods and Supplements" on page 230 for a few who do. Just follow the dosage information on the label. But, if you can't find the herb that you're looking for in a product designed for dogs, simply buy one for people at a health food store. Use the following guidelines as a starting point to adapt the dosages for your dog:

Capsules: One 500-milligram capsule for each 25 pounds your dog weighs, given two to three times daily.

Powders: ½ to 1 teaspoon of powder for each 25 pounds your dog weighs, given two to three times daily.

Tinctures: 5 to 10 drops for each 10 pounds your dog weighs, given two to three times daily.

Fresh herbs: 4 grams of fresh herbs for each 20 pounds your dog weighs, given two to three times daily.

he or she would do when using conventional deworming medicines.

Keep in mind that some of these intestinal parasites, such as giardiasis, hookworms, and roundworms, can be transmitted to people. Proper therapy is important, as is using good hygiene to prevent infections in people. If your pet is diagnosed with one of these parasites, ask your veterinarian how to prevent infection in people.

WRAPPING UP

As we end Week 2 of our 8 Weeks to a Healthy Dog Program, your dog should be free of parasites. If you worry about them coming back, you should put a preventive plan in place to keep your pet free of parasites so he can continue on the road to health. (I think this is a wise plan for every dog.)

Now let's turn our attention to Week 3, where you will learn how to choose the best diet for your pet. Since "we are what we eat"—and your pet is what she eats, too!—you won't want to skip this very important part of the 8-Week Program.

ASK DR. SHAWN

Dear Dr. Shawn: "I like to avoid giving my dog drugs whenever possible. Please tell me, are there any natural alternatives for heartworms?"

A: Treating heartworms with natural means is very controversial. I have not seen any proven therapies, despite several anecdotal observations that have been reported. The recommended natural therapies usually include the herb black walnut. Here are some of the concerns I have with the reports I have read.

Whenever I read of successful treatment of heartworms using natural therapies, my first question is: How was the dog diagnosed with this disease? Did the doctor diagnose heartworms by examining a drop of blood under the microscope (which is a totally inaccurate test), by using a filter or concentration test (which detects only the microfilariae and not the adult heartworms), or by using an antigen test (which detects the presence of adult female heartworms)? If I don't know how the disease was diagnosed, I'm not convinced the dog actually had heartworms. So then, when the report says the natural therapy worked, I'm not convinced because I'm not sure the dog really had heartworms to begin with.

My second question is: Was another antigen test done four months after treatment to prove success? That's the only way I would be convinced that the treatment worked.

My third question is: Were any other drugs used that might have contributed to the success of the therapy? For example, if the pet was given an alternative therapy but also placed on the monthly preventive drug ivermectin, most likely the drug, not the alternative therapy, cured the heartworms.

I've read some reports where doctors tried using black walnut for heartworms. The doctors admitted that the black walnut didn't work, so then they gave the dog a conventional drug. When the conventional drug got rid of the worms, the doctors claimed that the black walnut "weakened" the heartworms, making conventional medication more effective. Ha! Sounds great, but I have no idea how to prove such an assertion.

The bottom line is, I would love to recommend a natural therapy for heartworms in place of the conventional drugs we currently use. But the truth is, I am unable to confidently do so until we have definitive proof that any natural therapies work as well as the conventional medications.

5

WEEK 3:
Choosing the Best Diet
for Your Dog

D iet is so important to our pets' health and well-being, yet it's easy to overlook. This is unfortunate because, after all, our dogs eat every day. Plus, because your dog's diet is totally under your control, it is the *one* variable in our 8 Weeks to a Healthy Dog Program of good health that you can always control to make a difference in your dog's life. In "Week 4: Choosing Nutritional Supplements for Your Dog," I'll discuss how nutritional supplements can improve your pet's health. But consider this: No matter what supplement may be important in helping your dog overcome disease and maintain good health, if he is not fed the proper diet, that supplement will never be able to exert its maximum effect.

Diet really *is* that important, so I want you to stop and think about what you are currently feeding your dog. Do you know what's in the food you feed? Do you really know what your dog had for dinner last night? Was it a healthy, wholesome, nutritious meal? Or was it the least expensive bag or can of food you could find at the store? Maybe it was a brand recommended by your doctor or local pet store clerk, or possibly it was the latest fad diet, promoted with splashy advertisements in major popular publications.

The sad fact is that most of us don't have a clue what we're feeding our pets, yet we seem surprised when the food we put into their bodies every day fails to maintain health! When you consider that it is estimated that at least 50 percent of the diseases diagnosed

DR. SHAWN SAYS

I'm going to spell it out one more time: Diet is the least expensive and easiest variable that you can control to determine the degree of health (or lack of health) your dog will have throughout his entire life. Make sure your dog's eating right!

in people and pets can be prevented with proper diet and supplementation, it's easy to appreciate just how important selecting and feeding the best diet is for your pet's health.

With the information you will learn in this chapter, you'll be able to make an important decision that will affect your pet's health for the rest of his life. By the end of the chapter, you will be able to select (or prepare at home, if you choose) the most nutritious diet you can find to meet your dog's individual needs.

I'm sure that, like most pet owners, you probably feel that you are currently feeding your dog the absolute best diet you could find. However, in my practice I see a number of dogs that really aren't eating what I would consider the best or most healthy diet.

It may seem simple—just buy a bag or can—but it's really quite difficult to know what your pet should eat. Owners and doctors are bombarded with advertisements telling us what food we should feed our pets and recommend to our clients. Usually, owners choose a diet based on the claims in the ads and the price of the food, rather than on nutritional content.

I certainly encourage you to consult with your pet's doctor to find the best diet for him. This is particularly true if your dog has a medical condition and needs a prescribed, medicated diet. However, to avoid any prejudices by doctors, it is ultimately up to pet owners to read the label and find the best premium food for their pets.

A homemade diet (for example, one made from the recipes included later in this chapter) may be the best choice for your dog because a homemade diet is prepared fresh from wholesome cooked or raw ingredients. This is particularly true if you purchase and prepare organic produce for your pet. However, since most owners don't have the time to prepare pet food, a quality premium diet (properly supplemented with healthy nutritional supplements, which we'll discuss in Week 4) is the next-best option.

WHAT'S IN THE BAG?

There are many fine brands of dog food, and I certainly don't want to recommend one over another. (You'll find some well-known "natural" brands listed in "Popular Brands of Natural Diets" on page 76.) But I *do* want to encourage you to learn to read labels so you can tell what might be an appropriately healthy food for your dog. While labels can be confusing at first glance (and some of the terms on the label can be misleading, even when you understand the true definitions of the terms), I'll help you begin to appreciate what really is included in your dog's processed dry or canned diet.

Look at the Label

Okay, confess: Have you ever read a dog-food label before? You'd be surprised at how much information you can learn from reading the labels on cans and bags of dog food. Just as you'd see a big difference between the ingredients list on a package of Twinkies and on a loaf of whole grain bread, you'll find that there are major differences between different brands of pet food in terms of quality and nutritional

DR. SHAWN'S TRICKS OF THE TRADE

To keep your dog interested in the diet you select, I recommend rotating among several brands every few months as I do for my Cavalier King Charles spaniel, Rita. (Would *you* want to eat the same food every day for 20 years?) If your dog has a particularly sensitive gastrointestinal system, just be sure to mix the new brand of food with the old one for a few days to wean your pet onto the new brand, rather than switching diets suddenly.

Popular Brands of Natural Diets

The diets in this list are among those most often prescribed for healthy pets by holistic doctors. Since companies can and do change ingredients, it is important to contact the manufacturer if a term appears on the food label that might be confusing. Also, I encourage you to check with your veterinarian to see if a new diet that might be better has been introduced.

AvoDerm	PetGuard
California Natural/Innova	PHD
CANIDAE	Pinnacle
Eagle Pack Holistic Select	Precise
Flint River Ranch	Royal Canin Natural Blend
Lick Your Chops	Sensible Choice
Muenster Natural Dog Food	Solid Gold
Nature's Variety	Wellness
Nutro	Wysong

You'll notice that this list of natural diets does not include Eukanuba, Gaines, Hill's, Iams, Purina, or other well-known names. As a rule, the diets made by these companies are more likely to use byproducts as the primary protein source, as well as various chemical preservatives and additives. While some medicated ("prescription") diets made by these companies might be more "wholesome" than their maintenance diets, and while they are often very useful as part of the therapy for pets with various diseases, such as heart disease, obesity, and kidney disease, the medicated diets may also contain byproducts and chemicals. If a medicated diet is truly required as part of the therapy for a disease, and a pet owner is unable to prepare such a diet at home, I will usually prescribe the medicated food. I believe their positive attributes, such as less sodium and decreased levels of protein, outweigh their faults.

value. I show you how to read labels step-by-step in "How to Read a Pet Food Label" on page 197, including how to determine the quality of the ingredients, which ingredient makes up the bulk of the food (it's not always the one that's listed first), what the more obscure words mean (try saying "ethylenediamine dihydroiodide" three times fast!), and how to tell how the food's preserved. (Some preservatives are far more healthy than others.)

Here are three points to consider as you read dog food labels:

1. The diet should contain a minimal amount or no byproducts.

2. Chemical preservatives and additives really have no place in your pet's healthy diet. Instead, look for food with natural preservatives, such as vitamins C and E.

3. The type of protein used in your dog's food, whether it's beef, chicken, or lamb, really makes no difference to your pet. And despite advertisements to the contrary, "lamb and rice" diets are not hypoallergenic and offer no special benefits to dogs.

I urge you to be an informed dog-food shopper, and look at the labels first and the price tags second. Your dog's health—and ultimately, his happiness—are at stake! But labels can't say everything. While reading a label can provide valuable information, you may still need to ask the manufacturer specific questions before you make your final choice. Do the best you can, and try to find the healthiest, most natural diet for your pet.

DR. SHAWN'S TRICKS OF THE TRADE

There is a secret to switching your dog to a new, healthier diet. Switching to a new food overnight may cause vomiting or diarrhea in a few dogs; some pets are finicky and may not even eat a new diet that is suddenly introduced. The best way to offer your dog a new diet is by gradually introducing him to it. Here's how: When you have about a week's worth of the old diet remaining, purchase or prepare the new, healthier diet. Add about 10 percent of the new diet each day for five to seven days, gradually adding more until you run out of the old food and your dog is eating only the new diet. This trick should acclimate your dog to the new food's flavor and texture gradually and prevent the digestive upsets that may occur if you switch foods suddenly.

What about Prescription Diets?

There's a reason I've focused on diet in Week 3 of our program, rather than earlier. Your doctor can't possibly recommend the best food for your dog until after he or she obtains necessary information concerning your pet's health. That includes the results from the physical examination and laboratory testing that he or she has performed in Week 1 of our program.

Most dogs, after having received their examination and laboratory tests in Week 1, will probably check out fine and not need a therapeutic (medicated, prescription) diet. But there are dogs who, because of aging or health problems detected in Week 1, will need a diet designed especially for them. Your doctor can make a recommendation after determining the state of your pet's health during the Week 1 evaluation.

In general, obese pets need a high-fiber diet. Pets with kidney or heart conditions need a diet composed of high-quality, easily digestible protein and decreased amounts of sodium and phosphorus. Dogs with gastrointestinal problems usually do best when fed low-fat diets containing easily digestible carbohydrates. And pets with food allergies will require a hypoallergenic diet.

As I mentioned in "Popular Brands of Natural Diets" on page 76, some of the prescription or medicated diets may contain less than desirable ingredients, including by-products and chemicals. I am often asked if it is okay to feed these diets, since they are not as "healthy" and natural as the ones I recommend for the 8 Weeks to a Healthy Dog Program. Whenever you can, I prefer that you prepare a diet, even a medicated or prescription diet, for your pet at home. (You'll find many good recipes for prescription diets in my book the *Natural Health Bible for Dogs & Cats.*) But I know that cooking for dogs is often difficult for many pet owners, and if you don't have time to cook for your pet, a prescription or medicated diet from your veterinarian is a viable alternative.

While the processed prescription-type diets may have less than desirable ingredients, I still recommend them. The reason is simple: I think there is more benefit from feeding a diet formulated for your pet's medical condition than the slight harm that might come from the less desirable ingredients contained in the diet. Your pet is much more likely to become sicker or even die from a medical condition than he is from eating a food that is not quite perfect. While I encourage pet owners to feed their dogs the best possible diet, the most holistic approach is to feed the best possible diet for *your* pet's needs. It's good for all of us to use some common sense here and not over-react. I think we all need to not worry and panic over every little thing but simply do the best we can.

Taking this attitude with your dog will help you relax and enjoy your pet more. For example, a pet dying of cancer should be fed the appropriate diet whenever possible. However, if the pet won't eat the best recommended diet but will only eat the not-so-healthy generic diet he's always eaten, don't make a big deal about it. Your pet needs to eat, and making his last few months as happy as possible is much more important than starving him until he reluctantly takes a few bites of the "better" but less preferred food. Use this chapter as a guideline, but remember, your pet has to eat whatever diet you choose to feed.

To Treat, or Not to Treat?

Before we get to homemade foods and recipes, let's talk about treats. Most owners like to feed their dogs treats. As with many diets, the ingredients used in many commercially available treats are not always of the highest quality. And dogs that are eating medically controlled diets don't need the extra calories or sodium that may be present in some treats.

As with selecting the proper diet for your pet, I recommend working with your doctor to find the appropriate treat. Keep in mind that most pets do not need treats any more than we need snacks or desserts. In most cases that I have encountered, it was the owners

On the Case with Dr. Shawn

LYNN

Here's a case where a prescription or medicated food was the best solution. I first saw Lynn, a one-year-old spayed female Shih Tzu, for evaluation of kidney disease. In analyzing her blood tests, I noticed that her BUN (blood urea nitrogen) and creatinine levels were moderately elevated. These blood parameters normally increase only in dogs with kidney disease or kidney failure. Since young dogs are not normally afflicted with kidney disease, I wondered if there could be a mistake in the tests. Still, any abnormal value needs to be investigated, so I rechecked Lynn's blood profile two weeks later, expecting the kidney enzymes to be back within the normal range.

Unfortunately, to my surprise, they were elevated even more. Her BUN and creatinine levels were now more than double their normal values! Further testing revealed a congenital, genetic problem that may occur in Shih Tzus called renal cortical hypoplasia. There is no cure for this condition. All we can do is make the dog comfortable until the kidneys fail.

It's hard to say exactly how long a young dog like Lynn could live with this problem, but I knew it wouldn't be long if her kidney enzymes continued rising. So I placed Lynn on a special diet made for dogs with kidney problems, along with several supplements. When I rechecked her blood one month later, her kidney enzymes showed absolutely normal values.

At this time, Lynn is doing well. I will keep her on her special diet and supplements, and monitor her blood levels every three to six months. In this case, a special diet is able to decrease the amount of proteins Lynn's kidneys must process, reducing toxic byproducts, such as urea and ammonia, in her blood.

who "needed" to give their dogs treats. In some cases, the dogs were incorrectly trained using food rather than praise as a reward. When a dog expects food rewards for good behavior, owners must continue to bribe their pets with unhealthy treats to get them to behave or obey commands. This is why verbal and physical praise work better than food rewards when training puppies and dogs.

In some cases, dogs have learned to beg from the table, and owners feel guilty and reward the dogs with "people food" from the table. Since many of us eat unhealthy diets, we encourage our dogs to also eat highly processed fatty food by feeding table scraps. While it's fine to supplement dogs' diets with healthy vegetables, fruits, whole grains, and meat, they should not be fed from the table, as this encourages begging.

Assuming your pet does not have any medical reasons why she shouldn't have treats (such as diabetes, obesity, heart disease, or kidney disease), here are three ideas for healthy treats that your dog may enjoy:

1. Feed your dog a nugget or two of his regular diet if you choose to feed a dry processed food. This is healthy and can be done regardless of the dog's medical condition, as you are only giving him a small bite of his medically approved diet.

2. Feed low-calorie dog treats. Once again, read the labels to make sure the treat doesn't contain harmful preservatives and/or artificial additives. Even for normal-weight pets, low-calorie treats are ideal to reduce the chance of developing obesity. Keep in mind that just because the dog biscuit is low-calorie, it does not mean you can give your dog a handful every time you are inclined to offer a treat. To minimize cost and extra calories, I recommend breaking these biscuits into several smaller pieces and offering the pieces to your pet. That way, you're giving just one small low-calorie treat, but the dog gets several "treats" because of the small pieces of the actual biscuit.

3. Offer healthy human food, such as a piece of carrot or green bean (steamed or raw). These treats are low-calorie and nutritious as well. Raw vegetables (and occasionally fruit) are my favorite treats to recommend to pet owners, as they are the most healthy.

Remember: Treats should be offered only in small amounts. They are not meant to replace the healthy diet prescribed by your pet's doctor. Choose treats you can give without guilt, and then control the impulse to pour them on. Your pet will be just as happy with

On the Case with Dr. Shawn

BOSCOE

Boscoe is a 10-year-old neutered male Labrador retriever, and Boscoe is a big boy. As a matter of fact, Boscoe is what I consider dangerously obese. He should weigh about 80 pounds or so and have a body condition score of about five. (On a scale from one to nine, one is emaciated and nine is dangerously obese.) Boscoe actually weighs 105 pounds and has a body condition score of nine. Since we define obesity as any excess weight over 15 percent of normal, Boscoe easily fits this definition.

It turns out that Boscoe eats a popular "lite" brand of dog food. He also receives no real exercise to speak of and is rewarded with "people food" whenever he begs at the table. Whenever I see Boscoe in my office, his owner always makes sure she gives him at least three or four of the "doggie treats" sitting on our countertop.

Boscoe's blood tests were normal, except that his thyroid values were low and his cholesterol values were high, possibly indicating hypothyroidism.

I placed Boscoe on a severely restricted processed medicated diet plus thyroid hormone supplementation and coenzyme Q10, which can help with weight loss. I instructed his owners to stop giving him treats, especially people food. If they felt compelled to reward him for the begging behavior they had taught him, they could give him one or two pieces of the special diet food or a small carrot. I also asked his owners to take him on 20- to 30-minute walks at least three times a week. They were to feed him his special diet in three to four feedings each day, rather than leaving food out for him all day as they had with his "lite" food. I also instructed his owners to bring him in weekly to be weighed.

a couple of baby carrots as a boxful of high-fat treats, and he'll be much, much healthier!

PREPARING YOUR DOG'S FOOD AT HOME

Many of my clients prefer to prepare food for their pets at home, and you might decide to try it yourself. The only disadvantage of

Within two months, Boscoe began losing weight. He still has a long journey ahead of him, and I have to keep behind his owners so that they don't reward him with treats or people food.

Boscoe's story is all too familiar. I'm presented with a breed of dog that is prone to obesity, like Labs. The family leaves food out for the dog all day—as soon as the bowl is empty, they hasten to refill it so the dog won't be "hungry." The poor pet is not exercised. (Running around the backyard is *not,* as so many owners think, enough exercise for a large dog like Boscoe.) Many times the owner is feeding a "lite" food. Despite fancy advertising claims, "lite" foods are really not meant to help pets lose weight; they are designed to minimize weight gain in pets prone to obesity or in pets who have lost weight on a medically controlled diet.

While many pets will lose weight once the proper diagnosis and therapy is started, there are those dogs who are destined to be forever obese. Many times I suspect that the owners stop giving them their thyroid supplementation or persist in giving them treats. As with people, any exercise program that is begun is often stopped after a short period of time, either because of the owner's schedule or because the pet is still obese after a few weeks of the program. Pets don't gain weight overnight, and they won't lose the weight overnight. Owners must be very patient with dietary therapy for obese animals. The best choice is obviously to prevent the problem by working with your dog's diet to find a suitable diet early in life that will allow normal weight gain when needed. As a dog ages or his habits change, the diet may also need to change. If your dog suddenly starts gaining weight and his diet and exercise routine remain the same, consult your veterinarian right away.

preparing food at home is that you have to take the time to purchase the ingredients and prepare the diet. Otherwise, you'll find that there are many benefits when you choose to make your pet's food. Here are a few that come to mind:

• It's easy to do. Most recipes are easy to follow and take very little time to prepare. (Turn to page 87 and see for yourself!)

• It's healthy. *You* control all the ingredients that go into your dog's diet. There are no hidden ingredients and no chemical preservatives, additives, or artificial colors or flavors. If you shop for organic produce, as many of my clients choose to do, you truly can't feed your pet any better food. Your dog will get an abundance of enzymes, healthy bacteria, and whole-food vitamins and minerals with a homemade diet (something that's not possible without additional supplementation with a processed diet).

• **It's more natural.** Dogs did not evolve eating food out of a bag or can. While our pets are certainly far removed from their wild relatives, their nutritional needs are similar. Feeding your dog a diet similar to the one his wild relatives eat offers the same nutrients his body was designed to receive.

• **It's not boring.** Imagine having to eat the same processed food every day for your entire life! Picture yourself eating the same dry cereal three times a day, year in, year out. This doesn't sound too appetizing or appealing, does it? Well, it's not too appealing for your dog, either. If you feed your pet processed foods, at least offer a variety so your dog doesn't become bored. It's easy to change ingredients to add variety to your dog's diet if you prepare the food at home.

• **It's more appealing to you, too.** Many owners are "grossed out" by the sight or smell of processed pet foods, especially canned foods. Feeding your dog the same food you eat is much more pleasant.

I mentioned that making the time to prepare the diet is the only real disadvantage. There are also those rare pets that do not like homemade diets, and some have such sensitive gastrointestinal systems that they can't tolerate a fresher, healthier diet. But, unless your pet has one of these problems, preparing a homemade diet is the best thing you can do for your dog. The best way to make sure that your pet will like a homemade diet and not develop gastrointestinal sensitivity to it is to begin feeding it as soon as you get him, ideally as a young puppy.

What if you don't have time to cook an entire meal for your pet? Simply add small amounts of *healthy* "people food" to his processed food. I routinely offer my dog, Rita, pieces of meat, potato, and vegetables whenever I'm eating dinner. (Yes, I know I just told you not to feed your dog from the table! Instead, serve the dog a small portion in his dish either before or after your own meal.) Rita appreciates the variety of these fresh foods, and she gets extra health benefits from eating them.

What's in Homemade Food?

As you'll see in "Dr. Shawn's Diets for Dogs" on page 87, homemade diets have a great variety of healthy ingredients, and they're also quite flexible. I've provided plenty of substitutions so you can fix your dog a different dinner every night—if you choose to, of course! Many people find it easier on their schedules to cook up several days' meals in one batch, then portion them out at mealtimes. If you go this route, please treat your dog's food the way you would your own: Refrigerate it as soon as it's cooled down. If you're making meals ahead and have a microwave, your dog will probably enjoy having his meals "nuked" warm again before you serve them. But be sure to check the food's temperature before setting it down for him to make sure it hasn't gotten *too* warm!

As you'd expect, I recommend meat as a primary ingredient of homemade dog food. I think the healthiest meats for dogs are turkey, chicken, rabbit, venison, and beef. You can use these in rotation to give your dog a variety of flavors. You can also substitute other protein sources such as fish (I recommend salmon), low-fat cottage cheese, tofu, cooked soybeans, or hard-cooked eggs for variety. Since dogs are not designed to be vegetarians, most doctors prefer to use meat or fish most of the time.

Unlike cats, though, dogs aren't pure carnivores. They enjoy a wide variety of foods, just like people. So I also recommend including a portion of carbohydrates in your homemade dog food. I like to use cooked long-grain rice (brown rice is ideal), potatoes (baked or boiled with the skins left on), or cooked macaroni or other pasta.

And don't forget vegetables! Flavor, texture, vitamins, and fiber make vegetables ideal additions to your dog's diet. You can add ½ to 1 cup fresh, raw, or lightly steamed vegetables (carrots, broccoli, etc.)

for extra nutrition, phytonutrients, roughage, and variety. Most vegetables provide approximately 25 calories per cup.

Just like us, dogs need those tasty and nutritious extras to supplement their diets. I recommend adding heart-healthy oils to your dog's food. Canola and olive oil are excellent for boosting flavor and palatability as well as health. And don't forget the salt—a pinch of salt or salt substitute (potassium chloride) perks up food's flavor for dogs, too.

I add extra nutritional oomph to every home-cooked meal with vitamins, minerals, and other supplements. I recommend using a natural multivitamin/mineral supplement, such as Rx Essentials for Dogs by Rx Vitamins for Pets or Canine Plus from Vetri-Science. Follow label guidelines for dosage. In addition, I suggest adding bonemeal tablets (10 grain or equivalent) or 1 to 1½ teaspoons of bonemeal powder to supply calcium and phosphorus. For optimum nutrition, you can also add omega-3 fatty acids (fish oil or flaxseed oil), plant enzymes (such as Prozyme, which contains cellulase), and a super green food or health blend formula (such as spirulina, wheatgrass, alfalfa, and barley grass; Barley Dog is one commercial formula) following your doctor's recommendations.

DR. SHAWN SAYS

What are phytonutrients, you ask, and why should I be feeding them to my dog? Phytonutrients are chemicals derived from plant sources that exhibit powerful antioxidant properties. The method of action for these phytochemicals appears to be their ability to decrease oxidative stress by strengthening the powerful antioxidant glutathione, located in the liver. Carotenoid and indole compounds found in vegetables such as spinach, broccoli, and tomatoes have been shown to modify liver detoxification enzymes and inhibit tumor cell growth. Antioxidant-rich phytonutrients may help forestall cell death and help reduce the aging process due to oxidative damage. Which all means, vegetables rich in carotenes (beta-carotene and the like) and other phytonutrients will help protect your dog from cancer and help him stay younger and more active. Sounds like good reason to remind your dog to eat his vegetables!

DR. SHAWN'S DIETS FOR DOGS

Here is my favorite diet for your adult dog, and my adaptation of it for puppies, if you're lucky enough to be starting the 8 Weeks to a Healthy Dog Program with a new puppy. If your dog is used to eating processed food, add the new food slowly (as I mentioned earlier, add about 10 to 20 percent every 2 to 3 days) while reducing the amount of the current diet by a similar amount. Doing this will decrease the chance of your dog rejecting the new diet and will allow her digestive enzymes time to adapt to the new ingredients, which will decrease the chances of vomiting or diarrhea. Keep in mind that these diets are for healthy puppies and dogs. If your pet has a medical disorder requiring a specific diet, consult with your doctor to determine which diet is most appropriate, then consult my book the *Natural Health Bible for Dogs & Cats* to find a homemade diet to suit your pet's needs.

A Homemade Diet for Adult Dogs

Here's my pick for adult dogs. Your dog will love this healthy stovetop casserole!

⅓ pound (uncooked weight) lean meat, such as turkey, chicken, rabbit, venison, or beef; fish such as salmon; or other protein source, such as 1 cup low-fat cottage cheese, ½–⅔ cup tofu, 1 cup cooked soybeans, or 3 hard-cooked eggs

2 cups cooked long-grain rice (preferably brown), 2–3 cups mashed potatoes (baked or boiled with skin), or 2 cups cooked macaroni or other pasta

2 tablespoons canola oil or olive oil

¼ teaspoon table salt or salt substitute (potassium chloride)
  Natural multivitamin/mineral supplement

4–6 bonemeal tablets (10 grain or equivalent) or 1–1½ teaspoons bonemeal powder

½–1 cup fresh, raw, or slightly steamed vegetables (carrots, broccoli, etc.)

Cook all ingredients in the canola or olive oil prior to feeding. It can also be fed raw; see "What about Raw Foods?" on page 89 for guidelines if you choose not to cook the ingredients.

This diet provides approximately 964 calories, 34.1 grams of protein, and 49.4 grams of fat, depending on the ingredients you use. As a feeding guideline, this diet meets the daily nutritional and calorie needs of a 25- to 35-pound dog. Increase or decrease the recipe amounts based on your dog's weight; for a 60-pound dog, for example, you'd need to double the recipe. I recommend dividing the recipe into two meals a day for adult dogs. Feed less if your dog's gaining too much weight, more if he's losing weight. You can supplement this basic diet by adding omega-3 fatty acids, plant enzymes, and a super green food or health blend formula. (See page 101 for more about these.)

A Homemade Diet for Puppies

Puppies need greater amounts of proteins, calories, and vitamins and minerals than adult dogs. I recommend this diet for puppies up to 12 months of age for breeds whose adult weight will be 40 pounds or less, and up to 18 months of age for pets whose adult weight is estimated to be more than 40 pounds.

½–⅔ pound meat (uncooked weight), such as turkey, chicken, rabbit, venison, or beef; fish, such as salmon; or other protein source, such as 1½ cups low-fat cottage cheese, ½–⅔ cup tofu, 1 cup cooked soybeans, or 5 hard-cooked eggs

1½ cups cooked long-grain (preferably brown) rice, 2½ cups mashed potatoes (baked or boiled with skin), or 2½ cups cooked macaroni or other pasta

⅓ teaspoon table salt or salt substitute (potassium chloride)

1–3 teaspoons canola or olive oil
   Natural multivitamin/mineral supplement

4–6 bonemeal tablets (10 grain or equivalent) or 1–1½ teaspoons bonemeal powder

½–1 cup fresh, raw, or lightly steamed vegetables (carrots, broccoli, etc.)

Cook all ingredients in canola or olive oil prior to feeding. It can also be fed raw. See "What about Raw Foods?" on the next page for guidelines if you choose not to cook the ingredients.

This diet provides approximately 765 calories, 44.5 grams of protein, and 32 grams of fat, depending on the ingredients you use. As a feeding guideline, this diet meets the daily calorie needs of a 20-pound puppy. I recommend dividing the recipe into three or four meals until your puppy is four to six months old, then feeding her twice a day. Work with your veterinarian to determine your puppy's exact needs; the actual amount to feed her will vary based on her weight. (Feed less if your veterinarian says your puppy's gaining too much weight, more if she's losing weight.)

What about Raw Foods?

While I suggest that you cook the two homemade diets I recommend, some owners may wish to consider feeding raw food to their pets. A raw food diet was made popular many years ago by Dr. Ian Billinghurst. His diet is called the Billinghurst diet or the BARF ("Bones and Raw Food") diet. This diet uses similar ingredients (mainly meat and vegetables with fewer carbohydrates) to the cooked diets I recommend.

The idea behind a raw-food diet is that this diet most closely mimics the wild diet eaten by relatives of our domestic dogs. Additionally, by not subjecting the ingredients to high temperatures and pressures, as can occur with cooked homemade diets or processed foods, the food retains more of its nutritional value. Vitamins, minerals, and enzymes are all retained, which makes the diet better for the pet. Raw-food diets have been fed to many pets with little harm, and most pets eating a natural raw diet look great. They may also suffer from fewer problems that can be related to processed-food diets, such as allergies and arthritis.

While a raw diet can be beneficial for many pets, there are of course some caveats to consider before feeding such a diet to your dog, especially if he has been fed nothing but processed food for many years. Here are the major concerns:

1. Some pets simply can't tolerate the "richness" of a raw-food diet. Some dogs vomit, some develop diarrhea (sometimes with blood), some develop pancreatitis, and some become quite acutely ill. Whenever introducing a new food to your dog, especially if the food is a raw diet, do so slowly. Add 10 percent of the raw food to your dog's regular diet every few days, while removing the same amount of regular diet. Within a few weeks, you'll know if your dog can tolerate this richer diet.

2. Feeding raw bones can cause problems. While small raw bones (such as chicken neck bones) are less likely to cause problems than cooked, larger bones, any bones can create gastrointestinal obstruction if the bones become lodged somewhere in your dog's intestinal tract. Once that happens, your pet will have to have major abdominal surgery to remove the bone. Dogs can fracture their teeth eating bones. Also, broken pieces of bones can lodge in the hard palate in between the teeth and require surgical removal.

3. While it's not common, I always worry about bacterial contamination (*Salmonella, E. coli, Campylobacter,* etc.) and parasite contamination of any food, especially raw meat, eggs, or vegetables. Organically certified raw meat, raised free of chemicals and hormones, that isn't infected with bacteria or parasites is safe. Because there are many strains of antibiotic-resistant bacteria that are prevalent today, food safety should be a major concern among pet owners. There are reports of pets eating the BARF diet who then develop illness (such as salmonella-induced diarrhea) when the owner feeds raw meat (especially chicken) from another supplier or from a contaminated source.

If you choose to feed raw meat, it is important to do everything possible to ensure that the meat is "safe" and free from pesticide, chemical, and hormonal residues as well as parasites. Remember that you need to handle the meat at home properly to ensure that it stays "safe." Use the same approach you would for your family's meals: Keep food refrigerated when you're not preparing or serving it, and thoroughly wash and disinfect all utensils used in food preparation, including the chopping board, after handling meat. Most food poisoning results from improper handling at home, rather than a problem with the actual source of the meat itself.

Pork, venison, and rabbit should definitely be cooked, and I recommend that you choose only animal meat that was raised "naturally" (without antibiotics or hormones), thoroughly wash the meat at home, and maybe even prepare the meat by grinding it at home (to prevent cross-contamination with other foods at the local grocery or butcher shop). If your dog shows any signs of illness as a result of feeding raw meat diets, take him to be evaluated by a veterinarian at once.

4. Dietary deficiencies (mainly vitamin and mineral deficiencies) are more common with homemade diets than with commercial diets. Careful attention to proper preparation is critical to prevent both deficiencies and excesses of vitamins and minerals. Use multivitamin/mineral preparations designed for puppies or adult dogs. You can also add child dosages (for puppies) and adult

DR. SHAWN'S TRICKS OF THE TRADE

If you absolutely *must* add bones to your dog's homemade diet, here are some options.

First, feed the smallest bones possible. I think the best are chicken neck bones or chicken back bones, but again, I recommend checking with your doctor before feeding *any* bones to your dog.

Second, start with a small amount of bone material and work up to the BARF or Billinghurst recommended amount. (There are several good books on the BARF or Billinghurst diet, and if you're interested in feeding your dog a raw food diet, I urge you to consider reading these to get more details on these diets.)

Third, consider grinding up fresh cooked bone into a powder and making your own bonemeal. And finally, if you want your dog to get the benefit of chewing on bones, simply cook a big bone (such as a beef knuckle bone) that is too large for your dog to eat. As he wears the bone down, you can cook another for him.

ASK DR. SHAWN

Dear Dr. Shawn: "My dog, Shannon, is a three-year-old yellow Labrador retriever. She was diagnosed with food allergies in a recent blood test. Her doctor recommended a special diet, but she won't eat it. Do you have any suggestions?"

A: First, it's important to know that food allergies cannot be reliably diagnosed with blood testing. While blood testing can diagnose pets with inhalant allergies, it is pretty useless for diagnosing food allergies. Rather, a food trial (ideally using a specially prepared home-made diet) is needed to diagnose food allergies. The special diet must be fed for at least eight weeks, and nothing else can be fed during this time. If Shannon is found to have food allergies, you can feed her a homemade diet using a protein source such as rabbit or venison to help control her disease. Having said this, even if Shannon doesn't really have food allergies, all pets can benefit from a healthy natural diet. Homemade is best, as you can control everything placed into her diet. Even with a homemade diet, I still recommend supplements, as many of our ingredients may be lacking in all of the nutrients we expect. If you don't have time to prepare her a diet at home, there are several brands of holistic foods that you can try. Good luck, and most importantly, be patient as Shannon adapts to her new diet.

Dear Dr. Shawn: "I know you're a fan of homemade diets whenever possible. However, I recently heard that popular farming practices may be depleting vegetables and fruits of important vitamins and minerals. What are your thoughts on this?"

A: Many of my readers have asked about preparing food at home for your pets. While there are some good natural diets, nothing beats a

human dosages (for dogs) of human vitamin C and E preparations for their antioxidant effects. Add calcium in the form of bonemeal or calcium tablets (gluconate, carbonate, or the lactate forms are all acceptable).

5. For owners who choose not to prepare a diet at home but prefer a commercially prepared diet that is close to natural, read the label to check for quality of ingredients (fresh meat or animal by-products) and

properly balanced home-prepared diet. An important advantage to preparing meals for your pet at home is that you can choose the best ingredients available.

Many pet owners prefer to use organically raised plant and animal ingredients in their pet's food because they're raised without hormones and chemical pesticides and fertilizers. According to information from the *Organic View*, Vol. 1, No. 17 (www.purefood.org/organicview. htm), there is a great difference in the nutrient content of foods raised by industrial agricultural practices compared to organically raised foods. For example, they report that in an analysis of USDA nutrient data from 1975 to 1997, the Kushi Institute of Becket, Massachusetts, found that, when compared with organically raised produce, chemically raised vegetables had 27 percent less calcium, 37 percent less iron, 21 percent less vitamin A, and 30 percent less vitamin C. They also report that a similar analysis of British nutrient data from 1930 to 1980 published in the *British Food Journal* found that in 20 vegetables, organic vegetables had 19 percent more calcium, 22 percent more iron, and 14 percent more potassium than chemically raised vegetables. Additionally, a 1999 study from the University of Wisconsin found that 3 decades of the overuse of nitrogen in U.S. farming has destroyed much of the soil's fertility, causing it to age the equivalent of 5,000 years. Finally, a U.S. Geological Survey report indicates that acid rain is depleting soil calcium levels in at least 10 eastern states, interfering with forest growth and weakening trees' resistance to insects.

Because of these potentially troubling findings, I suggest that you do your best to try and find the most wholesome organic produce available to use in any diet you prepare for your pets.

lack of additives (look for natural antioxidants such as vitamin E and vitamin C and a lack of artificial coloring and flavoring). Supplementation with natural products such as brewer's yeast, fatty acids, kelp, barley grass, cooked liver, enzyme products, and sprouted beans or seeds are often helpful to replace ingredients that may be lost during processing. (See "Week 4: Choosing Nutritional Supplements for Your Dog" on page 95 for more on healthy supplements for your dog.)

WRAPPING UP

When switching from a lower-quality food to a more natural diet (cooked or, especially, raw), it may take some time to get your pet to accept the new diet. It will also take some time (usually four to eight weeks) for the new diet to work. So it may take a month or two before you see any positive effects in your pet (more energy, brighter skin and coat, healthier skin, decreased allergies or arthritis) as his body detoxifies itself.

In the final analysis, the choice of what to feed your dog is up to you. Regardless of how you choose to feed your pet, it is important to properly supplement your pet's diet to prevent deficiencies and ensure maximum health. Knowing how to properly supplement your dog's diet is the focus of the next week in our 8 Weeks to a Healthy Dog Program. I'll tell you all about it in "Week 4: Choosing Nutritional Supplements for Your Dog."

6

WEEK 4:
Choosing Nutritional Supplements for Your Dog

Just as you and your kids probably take your multivitamin each day, after you read this chapter you may be asking your dog to line up next to you for his supplements. This may be surprising—supplements for dogs?

It's true, all dogs need nutritional supplements: young dogs, old dogs, well dogs, sick dogs. This week, you'll work with your doctor to decide which supplements are best for your dog. As much as I would like to, I'm not able to talk with you and evaluate your dog's unique needs. But by learning about some of the commonly recommended supplements, you can work with your doctor to determine which supplements will keep your dog healthy.

Later in this chapter I'll present an overview of supplements I use for healthy dogs and for dogs with diseases. This is by no means comprehensive, as there are hundreds of supplements available. All veterinarians have their own favorite supplements; in this chapter, I'll share my own favorites with you. If your doctor recommends something else, don't worry. Just talk it over to learn why your veterinarian chose that particular supplement.

REALLY, SUPPLEMENTS FOR DOGS?
I don't blame you for wondering why your healthy dog who eats a healthy diet would need supplements. Here are four reasons.

First, as I mentioned in Week 3, many dogs do not eat healthy diets. Most of the dogs I see in my practice eat inexpensive grocery-store food. (I'm cringing as I write that—I hesitate to even call some of that stuff "food.") Obviously, there's not much nutrition in a bag of food made from the least expensive ingredients, filled up with byproducts and chemicals. Many other dogs I see eat premium foods that were recommended by conventional veterinarians, slick TV ads, or local pet "experts" making minimum wage at pet superstores. While some premium diets are pretty good—especially the ones listed in "Popular Brands of Natural Diets" on page 76—others are not much better than the grocery-store stuff. The only thing "premium" about some diets is their cost! This is why most dogs eating processed food will benefit from the supplements in this chapter.

Second, when dog foods are made, they're exposed to high temperatures and pressures that take out certain nutrients, such as enzymes and helpful bacteria, that would be found in the diet of your dog's wild relatives. Supplementation brings a dog's diet "up to par" with the one enjoyed by wild canines.

Our dogs' wild relatives eat a variety of fresh food that provides proteins, vitamins, and minerals in their most basic form. Wild dogs strip the meaty muscle tissue off the bones of their prey, then gnaw on the bones. In the wild, dogs eat the organ meats of their prey, which are chock-full of vitamins and minerals. Since wild dogs eat the intestinal contents of their prey, too, they're also eating predigested grasses and other plant material. Surely you don't want your pet doing any of these things! Supplements are a far better alternative.

Third, even if you're diligently preparing your dog's food yourself, you can't give him every single nutrient he needs at every single meal. Supplements are important to round out homemade diets as well. For example, it's easier to give your dog fish oil than to actually cook him fish, or to give him green food supplements instead of serving him algae!

And last, some pets, like my dog, Rita, are picky eaters. Rita loves her natural treats and any food our family eats. But occasionally Rita goes on "hunger strikes" and won't eat her dog food. Giving dogs like Rita supplements ensures that they get all of the vitamins, minerals, and other nutrients that they need. Some supplements that I add right to Rita's food improve the taste of the food and encourage her to eat.

Hopefully I've convinced you that giving your dog supplements is a very good thing to do. But as we take a closer look at supplements, you may find the choices overwhelming. There are hundreds of supplements available, as I mentioned. I recommend starting with just one or two. If your dog takes the supplements, add another supplement or two. If your dog won't eat the supplements, stop them for a few days and reintroduce just one of them at the tiniest dose possible. Your goal is to work up to the recommended dosage of each supplement.

But first, an important caveat: While supplements are very safe, and I have presented a lot of advice here, talk with your veterinarian before giving your dog *any* supplements.

SUPPLEMENTS FOR HEALTHY DOGS

Nutrition is such an important and easy part of health care, it's unfortunate that many doctors and owners neglect it. However, whenever I treat a dog using natural care, I spend a lot of time working with owners to select the best diet and supplements to help my other therapies work better. With proper food and supplements alone, we can often reduce or completely eliminate our need for harmful long-term drug therapies.

Here, we'll consider supplements for normal dogs. Later, I'll discuss some favorite supplements that I use to treat many of the diseases I see in practice.

Supplements for puppies. Supplements that can be helpful for healthy puppy are a multivitamin/mineral supplement, a plant enzyme supplement, fatty acids, a green food supplement, and a health blend formula.

DR. SHAWN'S TRICKS OF THE TRADE

The supplement industry has really taken off over the past few years. It's no surprise that the marketplace contains both good supplements and not-so-good supplements. Many manufacturers, dreaming of growing profits as more people turn to supplements for themselves and their pets, have entered the market. This means that there are many substandard products on the shelves of your favorite grocery and health food stores. Now more than ever, you need to do your homework before buying a supplement and giving it to your dog. Here are some pointers.

Give your dog supplements made for dogs. I am often asked if dogs can take the same supplements their owners take. It's true that with many supplements such as glucosamine, the glucosamine you take is usually the same glucosamine that your pet should take, but the dosages may be different, so you still need to consult with your veterinarian. Whenever possible, buy supplements made specifically for dogs. (See "Sources for Natural Foods and Supplements" on page 230.) If that's not possible, see "Doggie Dosages" on page 112 for some general guidelines to adapt a human dose to a dog dose.

Buy from reputable companies. Recent studies have shown that many supplements, such as those containing ephedra and glucosamine, do not contain the amounts of active ingredients listed on their labels. Some contained too small amounts of active ingredients, and others contained toxic amounts. This means that in the supplement industry, let the buyer beware.

I recommend asking your doctor which companies he or she thinks make the best supplements. Many holistic doctors sell the

Supplements for adult dogs. If your adult is healthy, continue giving him a multivitamin/mineral supplement, a plant enzyme supplement, fatty acids, a green food supplement, and a health blend formula. Consider adding antioxidants if your dog gets sick or as he ages.

Supplements for older dogs. Dogs that are seven years old and older should continue taking a multivitamin/mineral supplement, a supplements we feel work best. While they may cost more than generic supplements, they are made by quality companies that follow good manufacturing practices. Many of these companies also do the research and independent testing to verify the effectiveness of their products and verify the levels of active ingredients in their products.

Choose real foods. Some supplements are made with real food, such as wheat sprouts and barley grass grown in a field, while others are synthetic, chemically processed vitamins made in a lab.

The problem with synthesizing vitamins in a lab is that you're only getting part of the vitamin. For example, many supplements contain ascorbic acid and label it vitamin C. These supplement manufacturers are trying to pull the wool over your eyes! Ascorbic acid is *not* vitamin C; it is rather a part of the vitamin C complex. It's actually the antioxidant coating of the vitamin C molecule. While small amounts of ascorbic acid will not hurt dogs, unless there is a medical condition that would respond specifically to ascorbic acid, I would prefer for dogs to get vitamin C through a vitamin pill made of whole foods.

When you give your dog a whole food instead of a chemical, he's getting vitamins and minerals in their natural, raw states, similar to the way your dog would acquire them by eating a natural, raw diet. By providing nutrients in this form, your pet is assured of receiving vitamins and minerals as well as all of the extra nutrients and cofactors not found in processed, synthetic vitamins.

So look for vitamins that contain whole foods that you recognize or whole vitamin names, such as vitamin C, not chemicals.

plant enzyme supplement, fatty acids, a green food supplement, and a health blend formula. You should continue with the antioxidants, and you may need to increase the dosage. I'd add a choline supplement to try to prevent cognitive disorder (often called "doggie Alzheimer's disease") and consider coenzyme Q10 to help with many diseases of aging. You might also consider glucosamine and chondroitin to try to prevent arthritis.

DR. SHAWN SAYS

I recommend that older dogs take the same supplements as puppies and adult dogs. This makes sense, because they're still pretty
much eating the same diet. While some conventional doctors
make a big deal out of changing diets as dogs age, there is no scientific validation behind these recommendations. No matter what
you might hear, an older dog will not be harmed by normal levels
of protein, and feeding a reduced-protein diet will not prevent
kidney disease or kidney failure. These reduced-protein kidney
diets are best reserved for the pet with laboratory-confirmed
kidney disease or kidney failure.

So as you can see from these relatively short lists, adding just
these few, basic supplements to your dog's diet can really help to
maintain her good health. These same supplements are also often
prescribed for dogs with illnesses.

But please, don't get discouraged if you feel the list is too long
or the cost too prohibitive. Do what you can to make supplementation easy and cost-effective. Some pets won't take pills or liquids
easily, and there are some dogs that won't eat anything placed into
their food bowls that isn't processed dog food. You know your pet.
There is no right or wrong way to do this. Any steps that you can
take to help your dog, even if you can't give all of the recommended
supplements, are beneficial.

Here's some specifics on the supplements I've recommended, in
the order you're likely to introduce them to your dog. I've also added
my favorite sources for each supplement. You can order these
through your veterinarian or check "Sources for Natural Foods and
Supplements" on page 230 for the manufacturers' addresses.

MULTIVITAMIN/MINERAL SUPPLEMENTS

Perhaps the most important supplement you should give your dog is
a multivitamin/mineral pill. Giving one to your dog each day is a

little bit like buying insurance. It ensures that your dog has at least obtained the essential nutrients each day for optimum health. Your dog's vitamin/mineral pill is his most basic supplement. You can build on his individual needs from this point.

Dr. Shawn Recommends

Because there are several products made for dogs, I highly discourage people from giving their dogs multivitamins made for people. Our multivitamins can cause serious side effects in dogs, such as iron toxicity. One good dog multivitamin/mineral supplement is Nutritional Support. It's made by Rx Vitamins for Pets. This supplement is a mix of flaxseed, salmon meal, spirulina, bee pollen, kelp, and a number of herbs. Essentials for Dogs is another good supplement from Rx Vitamins for Pets. Canine Plus, which is made by Vetri-Science, is another option. A tasty vitamin treat made by Pet Applause is the easiest vitamin supplement to administer. You'll find ordering information for these companies in "Sources for Natural Foods and Supplements" on page 230.

ENZYME SUPPLEMENTS

A second key supplement I recommend for all dogs is enzyme supplements. Enzymes are used in the body for a number of processes. Without enzymes, our dogs' bodies literally could not function. Your dog has enzymes in his body, but he also needs to get them from the food he eats.

I tell the following story to illustrate how important enzymes are in the body. When I was taking animal nutrition during my undergraduate classes, our instructor told us that if we ever did not know the answer to a question on one of his tests, we should write in "enzyme." This proved his point that enzymes are an extremely important part of animal nutrition.

The major function of enzymes is to help digest and absorb food. This is critical for the vital nutrients contained in the food to be ab-

Giving Your Dog Pills and Liquids

It can be a challenge to get a dog to take a pill or liquid, whether it's a supplement or medication. Dogs just don't understand that they're good for them! Here are some ways to help make the medicine go down:

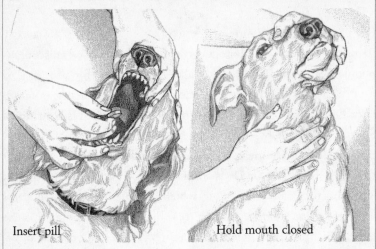

Insert pill   Hold mouth closed

POPPING PILLS

One way to get your dog to take a pill is to point her nose upward and pull her lower jaw open. Place the pill far in the back of her throat and close her jaw. Hold her mouth closed and massage her throat until you're sure she has swallowed the pill.

GIVING LIQUIDS

With liquids, the easiest thing to do is use a dropper or needle-less syringe to draw up the correct dose of medicine. Insert the end of the dropper or syringe in the side of your dog's mouth. Gently squeeze in the liquid. Work slowly, giving her plenty of time to swallow the medicine.

After all that, I'd say a dog treat is in order!

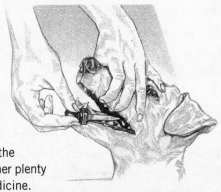

Squirt liquid in side of mouth

sorbed by the body. Studies have shown that supplementation with enzymes results in increased absorption of vitamins, minerals, and fatty acids, including zinc, selenium, vitamin B_6, and linoleic acid. When a dog absorbs these nutrients better, his overall nutrition is better, and his health is better.

You saw in the lists of recommended supplements on page 97 that I recommend that dogs take enzymes for their entire lives. One reason for that is that they're especially important for dogs that eat processed dog food, which is most of them! When dog foods are made, the high temperatures and pressures alter or destroy many nutrients, including enzymes. Enzymes break down at processing temperatures of 120° to 160°F. Giving your dog enzyme supplements makes up for the lack of them in her dog food.

But even if you shun the dog food aisle and make your dog's food yourself, she may need to take enzyme supplements. It's true that natural, homemade diets contain a number of nutrients, including live enzymes not found in processed diets. Still, giving your dog enzyme supplements makes sure that she's getting enough of these vital nutrients.

Enzyme supplements are also especially important for older dogs. Older pets are often picky eaters, so they may not get the nutrients they need. Plus, older dogs usually have fewer digestive enzymes in their bodies. These dogs need help breaking down plant materials, which are included in most dog foods.

Enzymes do more than just improve nutrition. Doctors often prescribe enzymes for pets with excessive shedding, dry and scaly skin, reduced energy levels, and digestive disturbances, including diarrhea, allergies, and arthritis. Veterinarians also often prescribe enzymes for dogs with illnesses or those taking medications, because stress can decrease enzyme function.

Once you start looking for enzyme supplements, you'll see that there are several different types, including plant enzymes, pancreatic enzymes, and microbial enzymes. I prefer to use plant enzymes in powders, so you can sprinkle them on your dog's food rather than giving her a pill. Because plant enzymes contain cellulase, I think they do a better job of helping pets digest the plant material found in our commercially prepared dog foods. (These enzymes are also found in the Pet Applause vitamin treat.)

But there's one important thing to remember if you give your dog plant enzymes: They do help your dog digest food, but they're not magical! They work best if they're used with a high-quality food. If the diet is not healthy, the enzymes can't change that, and your pet will not receive the full benefits from enzyme supplementation.

If your dog is healthy to begin with and you give her plant enzymes, you honestly may not notice any changes. But trust me, your pet is getting much better nutrition, and she will enjoy improved health and vitality because of the enzymes. This will help prevent diseases, fight off infections, and result in fewer veterinary visits for illness. So enzymes will save you money in the long run.

Dr. Shawn Recommends
Two brands of plant enzymes I've had success with are Prozyme and Shake 'n' Zyme.

FATTY ACIDS

Fatty acids are necessary nutrients for your dog. They are part of cell walls and help your pet have a healthy coat and skin. They're important supplements to give to healthy dogs, and in large amounts they are also part of the natural treatment for a variety of medical conditions.

There are two major types of fatty acids: omega-3 fatty acids and omega-6 fatty acids. These names refer to the chemical structure of the fatty acid. In general, omega-3 fatty acids combat inflammation, whereas omega-6 fatty acids promote inflammation. Inflammation is a bad thing. It contributes to many illnesses, including allergies and arthritis. So, your goal is to add omega-3 fatty acids to your dog's diet and minimize omega-6 fatty acids.

On the Case with Dr. Shawn
JO

Jo is a three-year-old spayed female terrier with digestive problems. She has occasional bouts of diarrhea and has difficulty keeping on weight.

I ran a battery of fecal tests to make sure Jo didn't have parasites. She didn't. I suggested trying dietary therapy, but her owner stated they had tried numerous diets and the one Jo was now fed seemed to cause her the least amount of trouble. Her owners did not want to try any harmful drugs on her. They asked if I could give Jo any natural remedies instead.

While I was concerned about the possibility of an undiagnosed whipworm infection or inflammatory bowel disease, both of which I commonly see in my practice, I respected their desire to try something natural first before resorting to drug therapy.

I prescribed a plant enzyme supplement for Jo. After only a few days, her current bout of diarrhea cleared up. Her diarrhea has not returned since starting the enzymes, except for one episode over a weekend when her owners ran out of the product. Once they got a new supply and gave the enzymes to Jo, her diarrhea was cured again.

Omega-3 fatty acids come from several plants, such as flax and hemp, and some coldwater fish, such as salmon and menhaden. However, the kind most veterinarians recommend comes from fish. This is because the fatty acids in flaxseed oil may not be efficiently converted to the active forms by our pets, especially those that are ill. Flaxseed oil is fine, though, for healthy dogs who are just taking fatty acids for healthy skin and coats.

Fatty acids from fish oil help dogs (and people!) with a variety of medical conditions. They have recently been shown to reduce the risk of heart attack and ventricular arrhythmias. While dogs don't typically get heart attacks, I believe the use of fatty acids is still warranted in canine heart disease. I look forward to objective research to support my gut feelings on this in the near future! Fatty acid supplementation may be especially helpful for breeds that are prone to a heart condition called cardiomyopathy.

Because they reduce inflammation, veterinarians prescribe fatty acids for many conditions that commonly occur in older dogs, including arthritis, kidney disease, heart disease, skin diseases, and allergies. Recently, omega-3 fatty acids have been shown to increase longevity in dogs with some types of cancer. This may be because omega-3 fatty acids can promote weight gain. They may also improve a dog's immunity, metabolism, and general health. They seem to keep tumors from forming and spreading. Finally, omega-3 fatty acids can reduce radiation damage to a dog's skin when the dog is receiving radiation treatments for cancer.

The catch with fatty acids, though, is that it takes a high dose to help dogs with illnesses. Many doctors recommend giving dogs two to four times the dose on the label to treat disorders such as allergies and arthritis. If you're giving your dog fatty acids just for overall health, rather than to treat a specific disease, the dose on the label is probably enough.

Dr. Shawn Recommends

My favorite fatty acid supplement is Ultra EFA by Rx Vitamins for Pets. Its combination of hemp oil and fish oil makes it pleasant-tasting for most pets, and only a small amount is needed when compared with similar products.

GREEN FOODS

Green foods, which are also called "super green foods," are wonderful whole-food supplements that are beneficial to your dog. The most popular green foods are alfalfa, barley grass, kelp, spirulina, and wheat grass. Some supplements contain one of these green foods, while others contain more than one.

Green foods contain a number of very healthy nutrients, including minerals, vitamins, enzymes, chlorophyll, and proteins. Kelp is a great example. This seaweed contains laminarin, which has anticoagulant properties and also decreases lipids in the blood. Algin, a polysaccharide in kelp, reduces the absorption of harmful toxins in the gastrointestinal tract. Kelp is also a source of iodine, potassium, protein, vitamin A, vitamin C, and other healthy nutrients.

Another great green food is spirulina. It's very high in protein and B-complex vitamins. It also contains potent antioxidants. Spirulina has numerous health benefits, including killing viruses, promoting red blood cell production, inhibiting cancer, decreasing inflammation in certain skin disorders, and supporting the immune system.

Here's a nice side benefit to giving your dog green foods: Some dogs, for various reasons, like to eat grass. Quite often after they eat it, they throw up. Supplementing these dogs with a powdered green food may help prevent this practice and provide beneficial nutrients in a convenient form at the same time. Plus, it'll save your carpets!

HEALTH BLEND FORMULAS

One last supplement I recommend for all dogs, even puppies, is a health blend formula. These products combine a number of essential plant and animal nutrients in one easy-to-use powdered formula. Powders are an easy way to give your dog supplements. Most of them taste good, so dogs actually like to eat them.

The idea behind health blend formulas is that the heat and pressure used when preparing commercially processed foods may alter some of the nutrients contained in the foods. Health blend formulas add back those nutrients that may be lacking in processed foods, including enzymes, protein, amino acids, fiber, beneficial bacteria that aid in digestion, phytochemicals that may prove beneficial in helping your pet maintain good health and assist in fighting disease, vitamins, and minerals. So they're excellent insurance for your dog!

ANTIOXIDANTS

Once a dog is full-grown, I recommend adding antioxidants to his daily supplement cocktail. There is convincing research that increased oxidative damage (damage to cells from free-radical chemicals) occurs with aging and is an important underlying contributor to many degenerative conditions, including cognitive disorder (doggie Alzheimer's) and cancers. Many different herbs, supplements, minerals, and vitamins have antioxidant properties, including vitamins C and E, the mineral selenium, the supplement Coenzyme Q10, and herbs echinacea and hawthorn. (See coenzyme Q10 on the next page, echinacea on page 111, and hawthorn on page 114.)

Dr. Shawn Recommends

My favorite products are NutriPro (made by Rx Vitamins for Pets) and Proanthozone or Proanimal (made by Animal Health Options). These companies make quality products and are committed to the veterinary profession and improving the health of pets. Dr. Robert Silver formulates the products for Rx Vitamins, and Dr. John Mulnix formulates the products for Animal Health Options. Both are doctors committed to making the best products available. The ingredients in the products are researched and are of human-grade quality. Either supplement can be helpful for a variety of conditions in which oxidative damage is a concern (which means I use one or the other product for just about any disease).

CHOLINE

At the age of seven, your dog is officially a senior. While becoming a senior dog citizen doesn't mean a membership in AARP, it *does* mean that more supplements are needed. The first one I recommend is usually choline.

Choline is a nutrient that's found in foods such as eggs, liver, and fish. It supports brain functions. I recommend it as a safe supplement to help stave off cognitive problems in older dogs.

As dogs age, they can have cognitive problems, similar to Alzheimer's disease in people. Studies have shown that choline levels are reduced in older dogs and people. We've found that giving dogs choline supplements can reverse signs of cognitive disorder. I've also observed in my practice that starting supplementation at seven to eight years of age can actually prevent cognitive disorder in many pets.

If your veterinarian suggests choline for your dog, the dosage varies with the size of the pet but ranges from a half-tablet daily to one to two tablets of Cholodin made by MVP Laboratories once to twice daily. This therapy has proven extremely effective in most pets. It's usually given for two months to assess effectiveness, although results may occur more quickly. Once your dog's effective dose is established, you should continue supplementing his diet with choline.

Dr. Shawn Recommends

My personal favorite choline supplement is Cholodin. I like this so much that I actually did the research on the dog and cat products made by MVP. I recommend it for older dogs and pets with seizure disorders as well because it often reduces seizure activity. It's a chewable treat, and most dogs actually like to take it.

COENZYME Q10

In his golden years, I recommend adding coenzyme Q10 to your dog's supplements. Also called ubiquinone, coenzyme Q10 is a powerful fat-soluble antioxidant that is located in every cell in the body. Coenzyme Q10 is a powerful antioxidant that appears to control the flow of oxygen within the cells. It also reduces the damage to cells from harmful free radicals.

Coenzyme Q10 is often recommended for pets with heart disease, cancer, obesity, and periodontal disease. These conditions tend to occur more commonly as pets age. Additionally, coenzyme Q10 levels decrease in both people and pets as they age. While supplementation with coenzyme Q10 will not necessarily prevent these problems, it is worth adding extra coenzyme Q10 to the diets of older dogs (and people!) as a protective measure.

GLUCOSAMINE AND CHONDROITIN

If you've ever watched an older dog struggle to get up because his joints hurt so much, you'll understand why I suggest adding glucosamine and chondroitin to your dog's supplements after age seven. These supplements can help prevent and treat arthritis and other joint problems in dogs, just as they do in people.

Judging from my own practice, many older dogs, especially larger breeds, have some degree of arthritis of the hips, knees, and spine. Conventional veterinarians give these dogs non-steroidal medications (NSAIDs) such as Rimadyl and EtoGesic. These drugs do work well to minimize pain and inflammation, but I don't like to use them long-term for pets with arthritis. I have three big reasons for this.

First, the NSAIDs usually cost more than joint supplements on a per-dose basis.

Second, the side effects from NSAIDs, which include kidney disease, gastrointestinal disease (including ulcers), liver disease, and the possibility (in some cases) of further destruction of the cartilage, make chronic use of NSAIDs potentially dangerous. I only recommend them in the very rare cases where no other treatment will keep the pet comfortable.

Third, because these side effects vary, veterinarians need to monitor dogs every two to three months with an exam and blood and urine tests. This sounds drastic, but it's actually recommended by the manufacturers of the two most commonly prescribed NSAIDs.

Natural joint supplements usually give the same amount of pain and inflammation relief as NSAIDs, do not produce the side effects of NSAIDs, do not require frequent monitoring of the pet for side effects as the NSAIDs do, cost less per dose, do not destroy cartilage and may actually heal the damaged cartilage, and also produce a residual effect that may last for a few days to a few weeks if for some reason owners miss giving a few doses, so I prefer to use these supplements for long-term arthritis therapy for all pets. I reserve NSAIDs use for acute flare-ups of pain that can't be controlled by other means.

Dr. Shawn Recommends

There are many joint supplements available. Some are good, others are pretty much worthless. As a rule, the less expensive a supplement is, the less effective it will be. Good joint supplements are not cheap, but they can be cost-effective. Rx Vitamins for Pets, Animal Health Options, and Vetri-Science make some of my favorite supplements. Rx Vitamins makes Nutriflex and Megaflex, Animal Health Options makes ProMotion and Prosamine, and Vetri-Science makes the line of Glyco-Flex supplements. Two new supplements called Cholodin-Flex and CholoGel by MVP Laboratories are also good options. I offer my clients a choice because some pets prefer a chewable pill, while others like capsules or powders.

SUPPLEMENTS FOR SPECIAL CIRCUMSTANCES

In addition to the supplements we've already discussed for healthy puppies, adult dogs, and older dogs, here are some of the supplements I most commonly recommend for dogs with various medical problems. (Be sure to check out "Side Effects of Selected Herbs" on page 217 and "Herb Interactions" on page 220 for important safety information before giving your dog these remedies.)

Echinacea

Echinacea, a common prairie wildflower called purple coneflower that's now grown in gardens across the country, is often recommended to stimulate the immune system and kill bacteria and viruses. All three species of plants, *Echinacea purpurea*, *E. angustifolia*, and *E. pallida*, are useful. Echinacea contains several active ingredients, including various polysaccharides, flavonoids, caffeic acid, essential oils, alkylamides, and polyacetylenes.

Echinacea modulates the actions of the immune system. It works in several ways. It increases the ability of white blood cells to kill disease organisms and stimulates the lymph system to remove wastes from the body. Also, by reducing the production of hyaluronidase, it promotes tissue healing and decreases inflammation.

Most holistic doctors recommend echinacea and other immune-modulating herbs whenever immune-system stimulation is needed. I most often use it for "tough-to-cure" chronic infections, kennel cough, and demodectic mange.

To prevent impairment of immune function, most doctors do not use echinacea for more than a few weeks. Then, if continued treatment with the herb is needed, it can be given again after a "rest" of a few weeks to allow the immune system to return to normal function.

While controversial, it has been recommended that echinacea not be used in cases of autoimmune disorders such as lupus or

Doggie Dosages

Even though lots of holistic veterinarians prescribe herbs for dogs, there aren't many companies that make herbal products specifically for dogs. See "Sources for Natural Foods and Supplements" on page 230 for a few who do. Just follow the dosage information on the label. But, if you can't find the herb that you're looking for in a product designed for dogs, simply buy one for people at a health food store. Use the following guidelines as a starting point to adapt the dosages for your dog:

Capsules: One 500-milligram capsule for each 25 pounds your dog weighs, given two to three times daily.

Powders: ½ to 1 teaspoon of powder for each 25 pounds your dog weighs, given two to three times daily.

Tinctures: 5 to 10 drops for each 10 pounds your dog weighs, given two to three times daily.

Fresh herbs: 4 grams of fresh herbs for each 20 pounds your dog weighs, given two to three times daily.

rheumatoid arthritis in humans and pets. However, a study in the journal *Alternative Medicine* questioned claims that chronic use of echinacea in people is harmful. Echinacea is believed to be an immune modulator rather than immune stimulator, and there is no evidence that it worsens immune conditions. More research is needed in this area to determine if there is a maximum duration of time that echinacea can be safely used.

Garlic

Garlic is one of my favorite herbs. It has many wonderful healthy properties, tastes great, and is one of the herbs pet owners ask me about most often. The herb garlic (*Allium sativum*) contains nutrients and sulfur compounds that have medicinal qualities, especially allicin and alliin. The sulfur compounds may increase detoxification enzymes in the liver, which might reduce the incidence of many degenerative conditions.

Allicin, one of the active ingredients in raw garlic, kills microorganisms on direct contact. Garlic is recommended to control intestinal parasites, including tapeworms, roundworms, and hookworms. Garlic has also been recommended as a treatment for asthma, diabetes, and high blood pressure. It can protect against free-radical damage, slow blood clotting, decrease inflammatory prostaglandins, stimulate white blood cells, and decrease blood cholesterol and trigylceride levels. It's used to reduce the risk of cancer and as part of the treatment for cancer.

While clinical proof in the form of controlled scientific studies is lacking, many owners report good results at controlling flea infestations by adding garlic and nutritional yeast to the diet. (See the section on fleas in "Week 2: Treating Parasites" on page 49 for other safe, effective controls.)

There is controversy regarding the proper dosage and form (tablets, powder, liquid, or fresh) of garlic that should be used. I prefer feeding garlic to your dog raw or sautéed in olive oil so he gets the full benefits of the whole herb. If feeding fresh garlic, I use one clove per 10 to 30 pounds of body weight per day.

Ginkgo

Ginkgo (*Ginkgo biloba*), another popular herbal remedy derived from a beautiful tree, contains many chemical components, including flavonoid glycosides such as proanthocyanidins, quercetin, and terpenes, including ginkgolides and bilobalide.

Ginkgo is used in people to prevent memory loss, increase mental alertness, and aid in the treatment of cognitive disorders, including Alzheimer's disease. It improves cognitive function by keeping platelets from forming blood clots, by improving circulation, and by strengthening blood vessels. It is also one of the few natural therapies for pets with cognitive disorder. Also, ginkgo stabilizes cell membranes and scavenges harmful free radicals, acting as an antioxidant. Because of its action on the nervous system, ginkgo can help pets with other nervous-system disorders such as seizures, incontinence, and deafness.

Veterinarians also use ginkgo for dogs with kidney disease because it improves circulation and antioxidant activity. And it's used for allergies because the bioflavonoid antioxidant chemicals in ginkgo may inhibit histamine release and decrease the production of chemicals that promote inflammation.

Hawthorn

Hawthorn (*Crataegus oxyacantha*), another tree-derived herbal remedy, is very useful in the treatment of heart disease and heart failure in people and dogs. It acts like the conventional medication digoxin, improving the heart's pumping ability. However, hawthorn also strengthens the heart and stabilizes it against arrhythmias. The drug digoxin can actually promote arrhythmias. Especially in the case of dogs with mild heart disease, hawthorn would be a safer alternative to digoxin.

As with other herbs, hawthorn also possesses antioxidant properties. Its active components are flavonoids and proanthocyanidins. The flavonoids appear to stabilize capillaries by decreasing the leaking of fluid from them. Hawthorn improves cardiac blood flow by dilating coronary arteries. Hawthorn acts as an ACE inhibitor, and in studies done in people, hawthorn appears to be as effective a cardiac drug as the ACE inhibitor captopril, which is related to enalapril, a drug that is used in dogs with heart failure.

Hawthorn is a very safe herb, and it's one of my favorites for most pets with heart disease. However, since its actions mimic digoxin, it is not recommended in the human literature to use it if digoxin or related compounds are prescribed. Follow similar precautions with pets.

Kava Kava

Kava kava (*Piper methysticum*), also simply called kava, is one of several herbs recommended as a natural sedative. Its active constituents include kavalactones, including dihydrokavain, kavain, methysticin, and dihydromethysticin. These chemicals produce sedation, pain relief, muscle relaxation, and decreased seizure activity.

Kava is a natural substitute for chemical tranquilizers such as diazepam and acepromazine and anticonvulsants such as diazepam and phenobarbitol. Unlike some conventional medications, kava usually does not impair motor function or depress mental function.

Recently, there has been concern about the potential for kava to cause serious and even fatal liver disease in people. However, close examination of the reported cases indicate that other factors may have been involved as well. To date, I have not seen any problems in the dogs I have treated with kava. In most cases, my kava patients are given the supplement only as needed for anxiety. For example, owners may give their dogs kava during thunderstorms or for separation anxiety. Regular monitoring of liver enzymes has not been necessary but can be done if needed. I would exercise caution if the pet has pre-existing liver disease.

Medicinal Mushrooms

There are several species of mushrooms, including reishi (*Ganoderma lucidum*), shiitake (*Lentinula edodes*), cordyceps (*Cordyceps ophioglossoides*), maitake (*Grifola frondosa*), *Polyporous umbellatus*, *Grifola umbellatus*, and *Boletus frondosus*, that I recommend for dogs with various illnesses. Please note: These are all healthful, edible mushrooms, not "magic mushrooms" or hallucinogens. Our goal is a *healthy* dog, after all, not a spacey dog!

Medicinal mushrooms contain polysaccharides, which may have antibacterial, antiviral, and antitumor activities, as well as immune-stimulating properties. In most cases, holistic doctors would prescribe any of these species of mushrooms for dogs with serious disorders of the immune system, such as chronic illness or cancer.

Some examples of disorders for which medicinal mushrooms might be helpful include internal parasites, demodectic mange, upper respiratory infections, lack of appetite, postoperative recovery, chemotherapy support, aging pets with any disease, elevated blood cholesterol, edema, liver disease, diabetes, high blood pressure, and bladder infections.

Dosages of the mushrooms vary with the product. I recommend following the label instructions. If you're giving your dog fresh medicinal mushrooms, I recommend four to six mushrooms per 25 pounds of body weight each day.

Milk Thistle

Milk thistle (*Silybum marianum*) is a very versatile, commonly used herbal remedy. I regularly use it as part of my arsenal for treating any type of liver disease. It can be used in just about any disease as part of the treatment because every disease affects the liver in some way.

Milk thistle is also very helpful for dogs on chronic medications to eliminate stress on the liver. Any drug can stress the liver, because the liver has to produce enzymes to detoxify the drugs. Some drugs, such as heartworm treatment medications (not to be confused with heartworm prevention tablets, which are completely safe), corticosteroids, phenobarbitol, and cancer medications, can be directly toxic to the liver. I'd consider milk thistle supplements for all pets taking these medications.

I also like milk thistle because there are no conventional drugs used to treat liver disease that help the liver heal. For most pets with liver disease, all that conventional medicine can offer are antibiotics, steroids, and fluid therapy, but none of these help the liver repair itself and heal. This is one instance where complementary medicine can actually offer a treatment that specifically helps a damaged organ for which there is no conventional counterpart.

The active ingredient in milk thistle is silymarin. Milk thistle compounds are usually prepared to a standardized silymarin content, typically 70 to 80 percent silymarin. Silymarin works by displacing toxins that try to bind to the liver, encouraging the liver to regenerate, scavenging free radicals, and stabilizing liver cell membranes.

In pets, the recommended dosage is 100 to 200 milligrams per 25 to 50 pounds of body weight twice daily.

Probiotics

Probiotics are very helpful for a variety of disorders in dogs. Probiotics are various healthy, beneficial bacteria, such as *Lactobacillus* species, *Acidophilus, Bacillus, Streptococcus bulgaricus, Enterococcus faecium bifidus,* and the yeast *Saccharomyces boulardii,* which normally live in the intestines and promote normal bowel health.

I recommend probiotics any time there is the chance of upsetting the normal intestinal flora, including before a dog has surgery, when a dog is taking medications like antibiotics and chemotherapy, and if a dog is suffering from any illness or stress. Probiotics may also supply nutrients to the pet, aid in digestion, reduce the presence of pathogenic bacteria and yeasts, and allow for better conversion of food into nutrients.

In general, probiotics improve the health of the gastrointestinal system in people and dogs. Probiotics apparently do their job in several ways. First, they produce chemicals that decrease the amount of harmful bacteria. Second, they decrease toxins produced by these bacteria. Third, they block the adhesion of harmful bacteria to intestinal cells. Fourth, they compete for nutrients needed for growth by pathogenic organisms. Probiotics stimulate immune function of the intestines, and they may degrade toxin receptors located on cells in the intestines.

Dosages of probiotics range from several million to several billion live organisms per day. Keep in mind that probiotics are living organisms. It's important to choose products from quality manufacturers to ensure that you give live organisms to your dog. Nutrigest is the brand I use.

St. John's Wort

St. John's wort (*Hypericum perforatum*) is an herbal tranquilizer and antidepressant. Its active components include hypericin and hyperforin. It appears that this herb may raise levels of serotonin, norepinephrine, and dopamine; cause binding of the nerve transmitter GABA; inhibit MAO; and act as a serotonin reuptake inhibitor; all of which maintain normal mood and emotional stability.

In dogs, St. John's wort is used for depression, separation anxiety, and certain forms of aggression. Some supplements combine the herb with other sedating herbs, such as valerian and kava kava. Recent studies in people show it is as effective as Prozac for treating mild depression. St. John's wort may be helpful as an antibacterial and antiviral agent, but more research is needed in this area.

I prescribe a dose of 250 to 300 milligrams twice daily for large dogs, 150 milligrams twice daily for medium-size dogs, and 100 milligrams twice daily for small dogs. Give it to your dog at mealtime to decrease the chance of causing gastrointestinal upset.

Valerian

Valerian (*Valeriana officinalis*) is used for sedation and as a treatment for anxiety. It can calm restless animals and relax pets who have trouble sleeping. It may also reduce seizures in pets with epilepsy, reduce digestive disturbances, and relax pets with fear-induced phobias. It can help pets that have anxiety during trips to the doctor or groomer and dogs with fear of thunderstorms.

The active components in valerian appear to work like the drug diazepam, preventing the breakdown of the inhibitory nerve transmitter GABA. Valerenic acid may also bind to diazepam receptors in the brain. Unlike diazepam and similar sedating medications, valerian does not appear to cause side effects such as dependency or impaired mental function.

In people, it is recommended to gradually wean patients off of valerian rather than suddenly stop administration of the herb (to prevent valerian withdrawal syndrome). I have not encountered this problem in dogs, but I would encourage slow withdrawal if the herb is used for more than a few weeks at a time.

WRAPPING UP

By now we're halfway through our 8 Weeks to a Healthy Dog Program. We're off to a good start! We've made sure your pet is free of parasites that could result in debilitation, disease, or even death. He's now eating the best supplemented, healthy diet—one you've picked just for him. Doing just this much in the way of health care, we have already gone a *very* long way toward adding a few extra quality years to your dog's life.

Over the next four weeks, we'll concentrate on treating diseases, keeping your dog fit and trim, reducing the need for harmful drug therapies, and helping your dog stay healthy with good grooming. Just wait 'til you see the healthy, beautiful, happy dog he's about to become!

WEEK 5:
Treating Diseases Naturally

What I'm about to say may sound ridiculously obvious. This week, we're going to treat any diseases your pet has. Well, of course, you might think. But the truth is, in my practice I see far too many animals suffering from conditions that have never been treated. I think there are three reasons for this: the cost, the owner, and the doctor.

Let's talk about cost first. Some owners complain about the cost of treating their dog's problems. Yet when detected early, most conditions are treatable if not curable. The irony is, the *least* expensive time to treat an illness is when it's first detected. The problem is usually less serious, for one thing. Also, there are usually more treatment options, some of which are less expensive than others. Natural therapies, for example, are usually less expensive than conventional ones.

If cost is a factor for you, be sure to mention that to your veterinarian. This allows the doctor to personalize a treatment plan that is within your budget. Talk with your veterinarian about health-care plans, payment options, and pet health insurance to help decrease the cost of pet care. You should never leave your veterinarian's office complaining about cost. Instead, work with your doctor to develop a treatment plan that is within your budget.

For example, I treat a lot of geriatric dogs. In addition to their annual blood tests, these older pets should receive an electrocardiogram, chest and abdominal x-rays, and urine tests. Priced individually, these tests cost about $200. In our practice, we offer a package deal and do all three tests while the dog is in the hospital for another procedure, such as a dental cleaning. Our current price for this package is only $45! This special packaging helps make the cost of preventive care more affordable. More than half of the dog owners in our practice elect to have these tests done each year regardless of the age of their dogs. It's a good idea because any pet can have an undetected illness.

Another common reason dogs are not treated for diseases is that the owners don't know about them. If you don't know that your dog has a problem, of course you're not going to have it treated. For example, if you don't look at your dog's teeth, you may never know he has periodontal disease. Similarly, if you don't check your dog's skin, you may not detect a tumor when it first appears.

Sometimes, even if an owner does know that his pet has a problem, he may not take the problem seriously. This often happens if the dog doesn't have any symptoms and "seems fine." I see this most commonly in my practice when I diagnose heart disease in an asymptomatic dog. During an annual exam, I may hear a heart murmur or abnormal heartbeat, which is also called an arrhythmia. Of course, I point this out to the owner. Because I am detecting a potentially fatal problem early, before the pet has symptoms of heart failure, occasionally an owner may decide not to treat the problem since the dog "acts fine." But this is exactly when the problem should be investigated and treated! Why wait to treat the problem until the dog is having difficulty breathing and can't walk? By that time it's too late: Irreversible heart and lung damage have occurred. The once easily treatable problem is now incurable and will result in the dog's untimely death.

The third reason dogs' diseases aren't treated is their doctors. I'm embarrassed to admit that some doctors do not do a good job helping owners have healthy dogs. These doctors practice the "run 'em in and run 'em out" approach to veterinary medicine. While some of these facilities are low-cost, others charge a high price for this shoddy treatment. If veterinarians fail to perform physical exams and diagnostic tests on their patients, those dogs will never get the treatment they require. Sadly, the owners will think everything is "just fine" because the doctors did not point out any problems.

Sometimes, these dogs make their way to my office when their owners request second opinions. The most common problems I detect during second-opinion visits, which other doctors have overlooked or ignored, are dental disease, heart disease, skin disorders, and tumors. I'll go over each of these in detail below, along with other common diseases that affect dogs.

Read on as we strive to meet our goal for Week 5 in our 8 Weeks to a Healthy Dog Program: to correct any problems that were identified in your dog's exam. Then, we'll continue our program with a healthy, happy dog!

THE MOST COMMON DOG DISEASES

Many treatments, both conventional and complementary, can be used to treat the most common disorders diagnosed in dogs. Since *8 Weeks to a Healthy Dog* is a whole-life program for your dog's total well-being, it's not meant to be an exhaustive reference of common medical therapies. I won't spend a large amount of time on this topic—I'll just cover the basics. If the natural treatment of pet diseases interests you, I encourage you to consult my book the *Natural Health Bible for Dogs & Cats* for a more thorough discussion of the natural therapies that are commonly prescribed.

Throughout this chapter, I use the term "complementary" therapies instead of "holistic," "alternative," or "natural." That's because in this chapter we're dealing with diseases, some of which can be quite serious. Sometimes, if a disease is caught early or hasn't gotten too serious, the complementary treatment will do just fine. But at other times, if your dog is farther along in his illness, your veterinarian will probably recommend a multipronged approach, combining conventional and natural or alternative therapies. In this case, the alternative treatments are meant to complement conventional treatments.

Many of the therapies recommended below are herbs. Before giving your dog any herbs, check "Recommended Herbs for Specific Diseases" on page 210 and "Side Effects of Selected Herbs" on page 217 for important safety information.

Let me now briefly review some of the more common problems your veterinarian might have detected during Week 1 of our program. For each, I'll discuss the commonly recommended conventional and complementary therapies. Chances are, if your dog lives to a ripe old age she will develop one of these diseases.

ALLERGIES

Allergies are genetic diseases in which the dog becomes sensitive to proteins called allergens. Common allergens include pollen (especially Bermuda grass here in Texas), fleas, dust mites, and molds. Unlike people, who usually respond to allergies with nasal symptoms, most dog allergies cause skin problems, such as itchy skin, hot spots, and poor coats. Allergic dogs often lick and scratch their skin until it's raw and bleeding. Allergies can also play a part in ear infections. Allergies usually occur within one to three years after a dog has been exposed to the allergen, so they're not often seen in puppies.

Many dogs have seasonal allergies, itching only during the season when the specific allergens are most prominent. Pets with seasonal allergies are much easier to treat and generally require lower amounts of medications than dogs with allergy problems year-round, who are usually more difficult to treat.

Certain breeds of dogs, including Belgian Tervurens, Boston terriers, boxers, cairn terriers, Dalmatians, English setters, golden retrievers, Irish setters, Labrador retrievers, Lhasa apsos, miniature schnauzers, pugs, Scottish terriers, shar-peis, Shih Tzus, West Highland white terriers, and wirehaired fox terriers, are more likely to develop allergies than other breeds. Because allergies are genetic diseases, affected dogs should not be bred.

It's probable that if your dog has allergies, he has skin problems. Researchers estimate that 25 to 50 percent of dogs seen in the typical small animal practice suffer from some sort of skin problem, such as dermatitis. Diagnosis is usually straightforward and treatment relatively easy. However, instead of trying to diagnose the cause of a dog's chronic dermatitis and itching, many doctors are content to just treat the pet with drugs. While the dog temporarily improves, he never really gets better. So, soon after treatment, the disease relapses, setting up the cycle of chronic dermatitis and drug therapy.

Here's how this cycle goes: The dogs itch, so they lick and scratch. This can cause bacterial or yeast infections. When dogs lick themselves, the saliva can cause bronzing—a brownish red tinge to the skin and fur—and inflamed and infected skin. Doctors prescribe powerful medications to ease the itching and heal the skin. The itching stops for a time, but it comes back after the medication has run its course. And so the cycle begins again with more itching.

Conventional therapy for allergies relies on corticosteroids, often called steroids, and antihistamines. These drugs may stop the itching, but they all come with side effects. Short-term side effects of steroids include increased appetite and consequent weight gain, urination and water intake, and very rarely depression or excitability. Long-term side effects include Cushing's disease, diabetes, infections, liver disease, obesity, osteoporosis, and suppression of the immune system.

Side effects are much less common with antihistamines. The most common one is drowsiness. But antihistamines don't control allergies as well as steroids. I believe the best use of these medications is for short-term, immediate control of itching, trying to limit their use to one week. I rely on diet and natural therapies rather than drugs for long-term allergy control. As always, I instruct my clients to use conventional medications only when necessary to keep their dogs comfortable.

Allergy Tests for Dogs?

If your veterinarian suspects that your dog has allergies, he or she will examine the dog. The diagnosis of allergy is usually based on an examination and by ruling out other diseases with tests, such as blood testing, fungal cultures, skin cytology, and skin scrapings.

Just as with people, it's possible to test your dog to see what he's allergic to. Intradermal skin testing is the best test. For this type of test, a veterinarian injects a small amount of each allergen the dog may be allergic to under his skin with a needle. If the dog is allergic to the allergen, a bump and redness will appear where allergen was injected. Blood testing, also called *in vitro* testing, is less accurate than intradermal skin testing for allergic dermatitis. It's not accurate at all for testing for food allergies.

Treating Allergies Naturally

My favorite complementary therapies for allergies include bathing, antioxidants, omega-3 fatty acids, herbs, and dietary changes.

Bathing. Simply giving your dog a bath may temporarily relieve his itching. Shampooing your dog washes away the dirt and particles that cling to his fur and soothes his skin. Some dogs get two to three days of relief from a bath. These lucky dogs rarely require steroids to control their itching. If your dog has allergies, bathe him every day or every other day until his itching subsides—usually within five to seven days. Then, bathe him one to three times each week as needed to control itching and keep him comfortable.

Choose your dog's bathing products with care. I prefer shampoos and conditioners containing aloe vera and colloidal oatmeal. I use medicated products with steroids or antihistamines only if the aloe vera and colloidal oatmeal products don't help. If necessary, you can use residual "leave-on" conditioners that contain steroids or antihistamines in between bathings to decrease itchiness.

Antioxidants. Supplements containing antioxidants have been shown to relieve some dogs' itching. Antioxidants inhibit chemicals, such as histamine, that cause inflammation and allergy symptoms.

ASK DR. SHAWN

Dear Dr. Shawn: "I've heard that I should bathe my dog only once or twice a year unless she gets *really* dirty. Is this true?"

A: Many owners have heard the erroneous advice that "dogs do not need regular baths" or "you shouldn't bathe your dog frequently." This is ridiculous! This advice may have been good years ago when our selection of shampoo and conditioning products was limited and dogs lived outside. These harsher products probably should not have been used frequently because they may have irritated the dogs' skin and caused excessive drying and flakiness. Similarly, most shampoos designed for people are too harsh for long-term use in dogs, as our skin is different from our pets' skin.

However, if your pet has any type of skin infection, seborrhea, or allergies, an extremely important part of therapy is frequent bathing with the appropriate medicated shampoo. When you begin treating your dog's allergies, your veterinarian may recommend bathing your dog every day.

Thankfully, we now have a large assortment of quality therapeutic products produced by veterinary companies specializing in products for hair and skin. These can be used quite frequently if needed. I recommend using a hypoallergenic shampoo and conditioner or rinse at least weekly to keep your dog clean and smelling good. Before starting a regular shampooing and conditioning program, talk with your veterinarian to select the products that will work best for your pet. Some products are too harsh for pets with "normal" skin and hair. Your doctor can guide you in the right direction.

I also believe a regular grooming program that will help keep the skin and hair healthy is important. Obviously, not all dogs need a monthly haircut. However, every dog will benefit from a regular program of shampooing, conditioning, and brushing. Daily brushing or combing helps prevents matting of the coat and removes excess dead hair.

Perhaps even more importantly, daily brushing or combing increases the bond between owners and their dogs. You'll learn more about the importance of regular grooming in "Week 8: Healthy Grooming" on page 181.

Two products I've used with success are Proanthozone, made by Animal Health Options, and NutriPro, made by Rx Vitamins. Follow the dosage information on the label.

Omega-3 fatty acids. Fatty acids derived from coldwater fish oil, specifically eicosapentaenoic acid (EPA) and docosahexaenoic acid (DHA), decrease some dogs' itching and inflammation. In studies, fatty acid supplements helped 10 to 30 percent of dogs with allergies. The response depends upon a number of factors, including the specific product used, the dosage used, and the presence of other diseases that may contribute to itching, such as bacterial or yeast infections or mange.

In addition to coming from fish, omega-3 fatty acids are also derived from flaxseeds. While flaxseed oil actually contains higher amounts of omega-3 fatty acids than fish oil, the acids are supposedly in an inactive form that dogs' bodies can't use. Therefore, most doctors recommend fish oil for treating allergic pets. (But flaxseed oil won't hurt your dog, and I have seen a few pets respond to it.)

Another type of oil, hemp seed oil, has been called "nature's perfect oil" due to its fatty acid ratio of 1:4 of omega-3 to omega-6 fatty acids. (Omega-6 fatty acids are a different type of fatty acids that are found in meats, nuts, and vegetable oils.) Hemp seed oil may be helpful as part of the treatment of dogs with allergies. One of my favorite fatty acid supplements, Ultra EFA by Rx Vitamins for Pets, contains both fish oil and hemp oil.

Whichever supplement you choose, I find that dogs with allergies need to take two to four times the label dose to control the itching and inflammation. Check with your veterinarian before giving these supplements to your dog. I have never had any dogs respond to omega-3 fatty acid supplements alone, so I include them with antioxidants and other supplements as part of my whole regimen for treating allergic dogs.

Herbs. Many herbs can help relieve itching in dogs with allergies. Some herbs are applied topically, such as aloe vera, calendula, chamomile, juniper, lavender, licorice, Oregon grape, peppermint, rose bark, uva ursi, and witch hazel. Other herbs are given orally, such as alfalfa, burdock root, dandelion, garlic, German chamomile, licorice root, nettle, Oregon grape, red clover, yarrow, and yellow dock. Talk with your veterinarian to choose which herbs are best for your dog.

Dietary changes. While true food allergies are rare in dogs, what you feed your dog can help his allergies even if they aren't food-related. Because all pets benefit from eating the best diet, I believe the most natural food is best for allergic dogs. I recommend that your dog's food be homemade if possible.

Some dogs show improved skin when fed a wholesome diet, even if they don't have food allergies. This may be because processed food can be contaminated with additives, chemical preservatives, pesticides, and/or hormones. Or it may be because processing the food removes nutrients from the diet. Processing the food also alters the nutrients. For example, heating foods to temperatures over 400°F causes an increased level of the more harmful type of fatty acids,

---

Doggie Dosages

Even though lots of holistic veterinarians prescribe herbs for dogs, there aren't many companies that make herbal products specifically for dogs. See "Sources for Natural Foods and Supplements" on page 230 for a few who do. Just follow the dosage information on the label. But, if you can't find the herb that you're looking for in a product designed for dogs, simply buy one for people at a health food store. Use the following guidelines as a starting point to adapt the dosages for your dog:

Capsules: One 500-milligram capsule for each 25 pounds your dog weighs, given two to three times daily.

Powders: ½ to 1 teaspoon of powder for each 25 pounds your dog weighs, given two to three times daily.

Tinctures: 5 to 10 drops for each 10 pounds your dog weighs, given two to three times daily.

Fresh herbs: 4 grams of fresh herbs for each 20 pounds your dog weighs, given two to three times daily.

which may contribute to disease. Plus, many processed diets contain increased levels of omega-6 fatty acids relative to omega-3 fatty acids. These higher amounts of omega-6 fatty acids can cause inflammation, which contributes to allergies.

Because feeding a wholesome diet is important and it's easy for most owners to do, choosing the best food is important for allergic dogs. Work with your veterinarian to determine the best diet to feed your dog if allergies are a problem.

ARTHRITIS

Arthritis causes swelling, stiffness, and pain. Arthritis is very common in older dogs, affecting more than 75 percent of dogs 10 years of age and older. But it can occur in any dog with joint instability. Arthritis most commonly affects the hips, but it can also affect the knees, shoulders, ankles, and elbows. It causes the joints to become inflamed and swollen and the cartilage between the joints to degenerate.

Just as in people, many different types of arthritis can affect dogs. The most common types are osteoarthritis and rheumatoid arthritis. Less commonly, the joints between the vertebrae of the spine can develop arthritis. This is called spondylosis and only rarely causes symptoms.

Any therapy for dogs with arthritis should reduce the inflammation in the joint and ease pain. Whenever possible, it should also slow down the progression of the arthritis and assist the cartilage in healing. While both conventional and complementary treatments can reduce the inflammation and control pain, only natural therapies heal the damaged cartilage.

Conventional veterinarians treat arthritis with either steroids such as prednisone, prednisolone, dexamethasone, or triamcinolone or non-steroidal anti-inflammatory medications, commonly known as NSAIDs such as Rimadyl or EtoGesic.

While very effective at relieving pain and reducing inflammation, both steroids and NSAIDs have side effects. I mentioned the

What You Must Know Before Using NSAIDs

While short-term use of NSAIDs is acceptable as part of the therapy for dogs on the 8 Weeks to a Healthy Dog Program, I discourage relying on them as a long-term solution. Most dogs with arthritis are older dogs. The manufacturers of these medications actually caution veterinarians when using these potent drugs in older dogs. Consider these facts from the package inserts:

Approximately 70 percent of drug reactions involving NSAIDs have been in older dogs. Older dogs are more likely to have drug reactions for several reasons. First, their bodies are less able to metabolize and excrete drugs.

Second, just like people, many older dogs take multiple medications. These drugs can interact with each other, increasing the chances of a drug reaction. For example, two drugs commonly given to older dogs with heart disease, Lasix and Enacard, increase kidney toxicity when used with NSAIDs. Also, pets taking both steroids and NSAIDs are more likely to have serious gastrointestinal problems such as ulceration.

Finally, many older dogs have medical problems, such as kidney or liver disease, that may be undiagnosed at the time a medicine is prescribed. These added problems increase the chances of a drug reaction.

It's important to keep these points in mind if chronic NSAID therapy becomes necessary. Thankfully, this is rarely the case. Most dogs can be treated safely and properly with complementary therapies instead.

many short- and long-term side effects of steroids on page 124. Side effects of NSAIDs include liver disease, kidney disease, ulceration of the stomach and intestinal tract, and possibly further destruction of the joint cartilage. It's best to use these medications only for short-term control of pain and inflammation. I rely on complementary therapies for long-term management.

Treating Arthritis Naturally

Complementary medicine has a lot to offer dogs with arthritis. Glucosamine and chondroitin, perna, and acupuncture reduce pain and inflammation and nourish and heal the damaged cartilage.

Glucosamine and chondroitin. Because they're usually used together, I'll talk about glucosamine and chondroitin together here. These supplements are commonly used for pets with osteoarthritis, and I believe they should be the primary therapies used for long-term control of pain and inflammation and to support the healing of the damaged cartilage. Unlike conventional medications, glucosamine and chondroitin help the cartilage rebuild and repair itself.

Glucosamine is produced naturally in the body, where it is used to make cartilage. But dogs with arthritis need additional supplements. Glucosamine supplements are derived from the shells of shrimp, lobsters, and crabs. Glucosamine is sold in three different forms: glucosamine hydrochloride, glucosamine sulfate, and N-acetylglucosamine. While all three forms are effective, glucosamine hydrochloride and glucosamine sulfate appear to be more effective than N-acetylglucosamine.

Glucosamine appears to be extremely safe with no side effects, except for dogs that are allergic to shellfish. Because glucosamine contains glucose, though, if your dog has diabetes, your veterinarian

DR. SHAWN SAYS

Here's an important word of warning. Before you treat your dog for arthritis, you need to make sure she actually has it. Many pets referred to me for acupuncture have been treated for arthritis without a proper diagnosis, so they hadn't improved on standard NSAID therapy. In many cases, it turned out that the dog didn't have arthritis at all! No therapy can be effective for arthritis if the pet does not have this disease. I see many dogs being treated for "arthritis" who in fact have neurological disease (quite common) or another problem, such as bone cancer (thankfully, not common). These dogs require different therapies for their problems and will not usually respond to NSAIDs. Because the conventional and alternative therapies for arthritis are so effective at relieving pain and inflammation and helping the dog walk better, any dog that fails to respond to therapy should be immediately reevaluated (or better, properly evaluated in the first place).

should monitor her to make sure her blood sugar levels remain stable.

Chondroitin also occurs naturally in the body. It is a major component of cartilage. In addition to helping heal cartilage, it also seems to inhibit enzymes that destroy joints. Chondroitin supplements are derived from animal cartilage, usually from cow trachea or shark cartilage. Shark cartilage may be especially helpful because it also inhibits the formation of blood vessels in damaged cartilage, and that diminishes inflammation. Like glucosamine, chondroitin appears to be extremely safe, with no side effects.

As with any joint supplement, you may need to give your dog glucosamine and chondroitin for four to eight weeks before you notice improvement. But unlike NSAIDs, improvement can last for several weeks after the supplements are stopped. Therefore, there is no harm if you run out of supplements for a few days before refilling them.

Glucosamine and chondroitin dosages vary, depending on the product. As a guideline, a starting dose of 1,000 to 1,500 milligrams of glucosamine with 800 to 1,200 milligrams of chondroitin is recommended per day for a 50- to 100-pound dog. After four to eight weeks, you can lower the dose to the level where your dog seems comfortable. This will save you money on supplements!

Perna. *Perna canaliculus* is an edible green-lipped mussel from New Zealand. It is a natural source of glucosamine and chondroitin, as well as a number of other nutrients. Perna is a potent but slow-acting anti-inflammatory agent that inhibits enzymes that can cause inflammation.

The recommended dosage is 300 milligrams each day for each 15 pounds of body weight. Perna is safe, except for dogs that are allergic to shellfish.

Acupuncture. A well-known complementary therapy for dogs with arthritis, acupuncture has been used for more than 4,000 years. Numerous reports in the human and veterinary medical literature show the benefits of acupuncture for the treatment of joint pain and inflammation.

We don't know exactly how acupuncture works. It may work by relieving muscle spasms around the affected joint, by releasing endorphins and relieving pain, by improving blood circulation to the spastic muscles surrounding affected joints, or simply by reducing the inflammation.

Here's what I recommend if you'd like to try acupuncture: Your dog should receive two treatments each week for four weeks to see how effective the acupuncture is for him. Then, depending on the response, increase or decrease the number of treatments as needed.

Other complementary therapies that may be helpful for the treatment of arthritis in dogs include sea cucumber, MSM, antioxidants, omega-3 fatty acids, magnets, SAMe, and herbs such as boswellia, devil's claw, licorice, topical capsaicin, turmeric, and white willow bark. Ask your veterinarian what he or she recommends.

Here's one last, general piece of advice for dogs with arthritis. To reduce stress on her damaged joints, if your dog has arthritis and is overweight, talk with your veterinarian about placing her on a weight-reduction diet.

COGNITIVE DISORDER

Cognitive disorder, erroneously referred to as "senility" by many dog owners, is a common condition seen in older dogs. Most pets with cognitive disorder are at least 7 years old, and many are 10 years of age and older. The exact cause is unknown. As pets age, their brains may become deprived of oxygen due to reduced blood flow, anemia, high blood pressure, and arteriosclerosis. Geriatric dogs also may have decreased levels of the nerve transmitter serotonin or increased levels of the enzyme monoamine oxidase B. When researchers look at the brains of dogs with cognitive disorder, they see plaques within the brain and its blood vessels that are similar to those found in people with Alzheimer's disease. In fact, this disease is sometimes referred to as doggie Alzheimer's disease.

Symptoms of cognitive disorder vary among dogs. They include deafness, sleepiness, housebreaking problems, lack of awareness of surroundings, lack of energy, and occasional lack of recognition of the owner. Sometimes these dogs just sit, staring at a wall. Without therapy, pets will continue to deteriorate. When their symptoms impair their quality of life too greatly, the dogs may need to be euthanized.

The conventional treatment for dogs is the drug selegiline, which is sold as Anipryl. This medication inhibits an enzyme in the brain, which leads to increased dopamine levels. Other medications such as serotonin reuptake inhibitors like fluoxetine may also be useful.

While Anipryl can be effective in some cases, the drug can have side effects, although these are rare in most patients. It also reacts badly with several other medications commonly prescribed for dogs, including Demerol, Prozac, Clomicalm, Elavil, and Mitaban. If your doctor does put your dog on Anipryl and it's effective, it must be used for the rest of the dog's life. This can be very costly.

Treating Cognitive Disorder Naturally

Several complementary therapies may help dogs with cognitive disorder. They include antioxidants, ginkgo, and choline.

Antioxidants. These vitamins and minerals reduce oxidative damage (damage to cells from free-radical chemicals) in your dog's body. Antioxidants may be helpful for pets with cognitive disorder because they protect cells in the body from damage by free radicals and stabilize the collagen in blood vessels.

Commonly prescribed antioxidants include vitamins A, C, and E and the minerals manganese, selenium, and zinc. Other antioxidants that may be helpful for dogs include bilberry, coenzyme Q10, cysteine, ginkgo, glutathione, grape seed extract, pycnogenol, quercetin, and superoxide dismutase. Proanthocyanidins, also called bioflavonoids, are naturally occurring antioxidants found in plants. (Another reason why foods such as carrots and other vegetables are an important part of your dog's diet!)

Talk with your dog's veterinarian about which antioxidants he or she recommends and the best dosages for your dog.

Ginkgo. Sometimes known by its botanical name, *Ginkgo biloba*, this herb contains the proanthocyanidins bioflavonoids and quercetin, both antioxidants. By acting as an antioxidant, ginkgo scavenges free radicals, especially in the nervous system. This may explain its recommendation for treating neurological disease in people and dogs, including cognitive disorder and Alzheimer's disease. Ginkgo can also inhibit platelet activating factor and prevent blood clots, and it strengthens blood vessels and stabilizes cell membranes.

Ginkgo appears to be safe, but because of its blood-thinning effects it should not be used with blood-thinning drugs such as warfarin, heparin, aspirin, and other NSAIDs such as Rimadyl or EtoGesic, which are commonly used in older pets with arthritis. Ginkgo should not be used in dogs with bleeding disorders or in those scheduled for surgery. (Stop giving it to your dog at least one week before and don't start again until one week after surgery.)

Choline. This nutrient is found in foods such as eggs, liver, and fish. It supports brain function.

I recently performed studies for the manufacturer of a choline supplement called Cholodin, which is made by MVP Labs in Omaha, Nebraska. The studies showed that choline improved cognitive function in pets with cognitive disorder. Cholodin contains a number of nutritional ingredients, including choline, phosphatidylcholine, methionine, inositol, and various B vitamins. I believe that early therapy can reverse most cases of cognitive disorder in dogs, and that choline supplementation may actually *prevent* this common neurological problem.

If your veterinarian suggests choline for your dog, the dosage varies with the size of the pet, but it ranges from a half-tablet daily to one to two tablets once to twice daily. This therapy has proven extremely effective in most pets. Therapy is given for two months to assess effectiveness, although results may occur more quickly. Choline is generally regarded as safe for dogs.

DENTAL DISEASE

The chances are very good that your dog has dental disease, which includes problems with a dog's teeth and gums and is sometimes called periodontal disease. Periodontal disease is the most common infectious disease seen in dogs. Almost every single dog I see in my practice initially has periodontal disease.

Many doctors don't make a big deal of dental disease. Some don't even admit that dirty teeth are a sign of a serious periodontal infection. I, too, used to be ignorant about the serious problem of periodontal disease. I was finally convinced when a cardiologist told me that the same bacteria isolated from the teeth and gums were found on the heart valves of dogs with heart disease. Since that time, I have made a very big deal about treating dental infections. As a result of early diagnosis and regular treatment, very few of my regular patients have serious periodontal infections.

Normal teeth should be pearly white without any yellow-brown tartar. The gums should be light pink, except in breeds with pigmented gums, such as Chow Chows. While it's true that most dogs have a noticeable breath odor (the dreaded "doggie breath"), pets with periodontal disease have *very* disagreeable odors coming from their mouths. These odors arise from months to years of infection, inflammation, and decay. Bad breath is caused by bacteria and bacterial toxins destroying the teeth and gums.

When the bacteria and plaque in a dog's mouth mix with the salivary film that forms on the teeth and gums, it can cause periodontal disease. With time, the plaque hardens and becomes the yellow-brown tartar (called calculus) commonly seen on the teeth.

Advanced periodontal disease causes excessive tartar on the teeth, foul fetid breath, loose teeth (from destruction of the periodontal ligament and surrounding tissues), bleeding and inflamed gums, and pus coming from the tooth sockets.

If your dog has dirty, infected teeth, get them cleaned as quickly as possible. Periodontal disease is an infection that can cause harm throughout the body, such as in the gastrointestinal system, heart, kidney, and liver. How does that happen? Because they are in the mouth, which often has minor cuts and abrasions, the bacteria from periodontal disease easily find their way into a dog's bloodstream, where they can migrate to other parts of the body and start infections there, too.

Periodontal disease becomes more severe as dogs age due to chronic infection, stimulation of the immune system, and wear and tear on aging organs that may not be able to handle the constant load of bacteria and toxins. It's critical that you treat periodontal disease early to keep your dog healthy.

The treatment of periodontal disease depends on the severity of the disease. Most veterinarians will treat dogs with mild disease with an ultrasonic tooth scaling done under anesthesia, treating the infection with antibiotics if needed. Severe disease often requires advanced dental procedures such as root canals, extractions, and gum surgery, just as in people. These are best performed by a specialist.

After treatment for dental disease, most dogs will need only an annual dental cleaning. Some may need treatment more frequently if the periodontal disease returns more quickly. In my practice, we clean the teeth of many smaller breeds twice annually, as they are more likely to get periodontal disease. Also, many of my older patients have diseases such as Cushing's disease, diabetes, heart disease, kidney disease, and liver disease. Because infections in these pets must be kept to a minimum to prevent serious problems, they require dental cleanings two to three times a year. You can help your

DR. SHAWN SAYS

Interestingly, many of the dogs in my practice that "act old," sleeping a lot or with decreased appetite, weight loss, and muscle loss, act like puppies again after their teeth have been cleaned. It's no wonder that treating the oral infection and removing the pain associated with it makes these dogs act and feel better. It's a real fountain of youth!

dog prevent periodontal disease by brushing his teeth regularly. (See "Week 8: Healthy Grooming" on page 181, for tips on how to clean your dog's teeth.)

Treating Dental Disease Naturally

In addition to regular dental cleanings, several complementary therapies may be useful to heal the teeth and gums, including coenzyme Q10 and other antioxidants, orthomolecular medicine, colloidal silver, and lemon juice.

Coenzyme Q10. This antioxidant, also known as ubiquinone, reduces damage to cells and controls the flow of oxygen within the cells. Coenzyme Q10 may help periodontal disease by decreasing the gums' inflammation, redness, bleeding, and pain. A typical recommended dose is 0.25 to 1.0 milligram per pound of body weight daily for dogs. The supplement can be given orally, diluted with water and rubbed on the gums, or both. Coenzyme Q10 appears to be extremely safe for dogs.

Other antioxidants. Antioxidants reduce tissue damage by neutralizing oxidative products (such as peroxide) that are formed when cells are damaged. Commonly recommended antioxidants include bilberry, grape seed extract, olive leaf extract, pycnogenol, and quercetin. These are given orally, applied topically to the gums, or both. The dosage will depend on which antioxidant you choose. Discuss the choices with your veterinarian and see which ones he or she recommends.

Orthomolecular medicine. This therapy uses high levels of antioxidants such as vitamins A, C, and E, and the mineral selenium. These are given orally, applied topically to the gums, or both. Some possible treatments could include vitamin A (10,000 IU for small dogs and up to 30,000 IU for large dogs), crystalline ascorbic acid (750 milligrams for small dogs and up to 3,000 milligrams for large dogs), selenium (20 micrograms for small dogs and up to 60 micrograms for large dogs), and vitamin E (800 IU for small dogs and up to 2,400 IU for large dogs).

Because these are high doses of vitamins and minerals, which carry the risk of toxicity, use orthomolecular therapy only under veterinary supervision. As the dog improves, veterinarians gradually lower the dosages to reduce the chance of toxicity.

Colloidal silver. Colloidal silver, a natural antibacterial, is usually applied topically right to the dog's gums and teeth. Quality varies greatly between manufacturers, so ask your veterinarian to recommend a product. Colloidal silver appears to be safe and effective.

Lemon juice. Some older dogs have stomatitis, a severe inflammation of the gums and surrounding supporting tissues. This may be caused in part by decreased salivary production. Putting a drop of lemon juice in the dog's mouth one to three times each day to stimulate saliva production and wash out the mouth may be helpful.

HEART DISEASE

I've already mentioned that some owners ignore medical advice when an abnormal heart rhythm is detected during the physical examination. Some doctors, unfortunately, tell clients not to worry about heart murmurs, rather than recommend early preventive therapy. Certainly I don't want a dog owner to worry, but I do want her to help me fix the problem. Heart disease is easily controlled in most dogs when diagnosed early, before the dog is showing signs of congestive heart failure.

I'm astonished at how some owners won't spend any money

when I tell them their dogs have heart disease based on my physical examination. Yet these same owners beg for me to "do something, no matter what it costs" once the dog is experiencing congestive heart failure. Unfortunately, I can't "do something" when a dog is dying, other than put him out of his misery. What a shame! *Please* let your doctor "do something" when he or she can help your pet and the cost is minimal! We want your pet around for a long time, too.

Heart disease is one of the more commonly diagnosed problems in dogs. The most common types of heart disease are valvular heart disease and cardiomyopathy. Either of these conditions can lead to heart failure over time if the heart fails to pump blood throughout the body and fluid accumulates in the lungs, liver, and other organs.

Valvular Heart Disease

The most common type of heart disease in dogs, valvular heart disease usually occurs in small breeds of dogs, when the pets get older. It affects 75 percent of dogs over 16 years of age. As dogs age, the heart valves can have structural changes that cause them to degenerate. The diseased valves thicken and pull away from each other, allowing blood to flow in a "backward" direction as well as forward. This abnormal blood flow causes "regurgitation" of blood. Your veterinarian hears this through his or her stethoscope as a heart murmur. With time, as the blood backs up, a dog will cough, and he'll have problems exercising as the condition worsens and congestive heart failure develops.

Cardiomyopathy

Another common heart problem in dogs is cardiomyopathy, where the heart muscle is actually diseased. This is most common in larger breeds such as boxers and Doberman pinschers, but an increased incidence has been reported in cocker spaniels. The average age of dogs with cardiomyopathy is four to eight. In dogs with cardiomyopathy, the heart greatly enlarges as the heart muscles progressively become thin and flabby. The diseased muscle fails to pump blood adequately, leading to congestive heart failure. While the exact cause is unknown, veterinarians suspect a genetic connection. Some affected dogs have been shown to have an L-carnitine or taurine deficiency and need to take carnitine or taurine supplements (or both) as part of their therapy.

Conventional therapy for heart disease includes medications such as diuretics and various cardiac drugs, including ACE inhibitors, calcium channel blockers, and digitalis. Not surprisingly, these powerful drugs all come with a high price: powerful side effects.

The most commonly used and safest diuretic is furosemide. This diuretic speeds fluids and electrolytes from the body. Dogs taking diuretics should be monitored for electrolyte imbalances, especially potassium deficiency. The risk of side effects, including kidney failure, increases when furosemide is used with other medications, such as aminoglycoside antibiotics, the ACE-inhibiting drug enalapril, NSAIDs, and steroids.

ACE inhibitors are the new kids on the heart disease block. Enalapril and captopril are commonly prescribed. These drugs lower blood pressure and improve blood flow to the body. Side effects include loss of appetite, diarrhea, and vomiting. ACE inhibitors should not be combined with diuretics. The combination can cause low blood pressure and kidney failure

Calcium channel blockers commonly prescribed for dogs with heart disease include diltiazem and verapamil. These drugs dilate arteries and slow the heart rate. This improves blood flow to the rest of the body. Overdosage of these medications may cause excessive slowing of the heart, low blood pressure, and heart failure.

Digitalis medications are made by purifying the active ingredient in the purple foxglove plant. Digoxin and digitoxin are the two most commonly prescribed digitalis medications. These drugs slow heart rate and strengthen the force of the heart when it contracts. Side effects include heart arrhythmias, vomiting, diarrhea, and lack of appetite. Dogs taking these medications should be closely monitored because there is a very small difference between the effective dose and the toxic dose.

Treating Heart Disease Naturally

Instead of, or in conjunction with, these powerful drugs, your veterinarian may consider one of the many complementary therapies that help dogs with heart disease. They include taurine, L-carnitine, coenzyme Q10, the herb hawthorn, and omega-3 fatty acids.

Taurine. Supplementation with the amino acid taurine may help dogs with heart disease, especially those with cardiomyopathy. Taurine isn't likely to help dogs with valvular disease, though, because they usually have normal taurine levels.

Early studies indicate that supplementation with taurine may be beneficial in American cocker spaniels and golden retrievers with dilated cardiomyopathy. Supplementation with both taurine (500 milligrams twice daily) and L-carnitine (1,000 milligrams twice daily) in a small number of dogs with low plasma taurine levels resulted in improvement in a few of the patients studied.

Taurine is safe to use in dogs. In fact, taurine is included in some patented herbal formulas for dogs with cardiac disease. Talk with your veterinarian about the right dose for your dog.

L-carnitine. This amino acid, which is also called carnitine, is an essential substance in the body. Decreased carnitine levels may contribute to dilated cardiomyopathy in dogs, especially in boxers, Doberman pinschers, and American cocker spaniels. Carnitine deficiency is difficult to diagnose, usually requiring a heart biopsy, and so it's usually not done in dogs. Carnitine supplementation at 50 milligrams for each kilogram of your dog's weight, given three times daily, or simply 2,000 milligrams given three times daily, may be helpful for dogs with cardiomyopathy.

While carnitine supplements can also be used for dogs with valvular heart disease, I'm not convinced it helps. However, as with taurine, supplementation will not hurt because carnitine is safe to use.

Coenzyme Q10. Research has shown decreased levels of coenzyme Q10 in the hearts of people and pets with cardiac disease. So it's not surprising that this supplement is very helpful for people and dogs with heart disease. Coenzyme Q10 is a powerful antioxidant that appears to control the flow of oxygen within the cells. It also reduces the damage to cells from harmful free radicals. Coenzyme Q10 assists the heart by helping it use energy more efficiently.

Veterinarians usually recommend coenzyme Q10 to treat dogs with any type of heart disease. Many holistic doctors use it as part of the therapy of pets with early heart disease, before heart failure occurs. It is one of my favorite supplements to use in dogs with heart murmurs, even if there are no other symptoms.

In dogs, the usual dose is 30 milligrams every day or every other day. However, many holistic doctors prefer a dosage of 0.5 to 1.0 milligram per pound of body weight given daily, especially in dogs with more advanced disease.

Hawthorn. The herb hawthorn is an important heart supplement. It may be useful for some dogs with mild heart failure as an alternative to the drug digitalis. Hawthorn improves the heart's pumping ability, strengthening the heart and stabilizing it against abnormal heartbeats. In people, studies show that hawthorn is an effective treatment for congestive heart failure and is as effective as a low dose of the drug captopril. Hawthorn may actually work in a similar fashion to ACE inhibitors. For dogs with mild heart disease and early heart failure, I prefer using it instead of the ACE inhibitor enalapril.

Like many other herbs, hawthorn has antioxidant properties due to its flavonoid and proanthocyanidin content. The flavonoids decrease capillaries' leakiness, improve blood flow to cardiac muscle by dilating coronary arteries, and help the heart contract better.

Hawthorn is a safe herb. I recommend giving dogs 100 milligrams for each 25 to 50 pounds of body weight twice daily.

Omega-3 fatty acids. The fatty acids DHA and EPA found in fish oil are being investigated for their anti-inflammatory effects in dogs with heart disease. Current studies in people show that they even reduce the risk of heart attack in people *without* heart disease. More studies are needed in pets, but since omega-3 fatty acids are so safe, I recommend them for dogs with heart disease.

In fact, I use them for just about *every* disease in an effort to reduce inflammation, which is a factor in so many diseases. I usually use two to four times the label dosage.

Dietary changes. What you feed your dog is critical if she has heart disease. Feeding a low-sodium diet can decrease excess fluid in the body. That's why salt is reduced in prescription-type diets designed for dogs with heart disease. However, these processed foods may contain byproducts and chemical preservatives. But they are better than nothing if you can't prepare a fresh, preservative-free homemade diet or if your dog won't eat a homemade diet.

Some dogs with heart disease have small appetites. If you notice that your dog isn't eating enough, talk with your veterinarian about potassium and magnesium supplements. These minerals can be deficient in pets with cardiac disease as a result of the disease itself, increased excretion from the body when the pet is taking conventional medications such as diuretics, or decreased appetite.

Other natural treatments that might be helpful include antioxidants, glandular supplements, and the herbs bugleweed, burdock, dandelion leaves, devil's claw, garlic, and ginger.

Having described some of the best complementary therapies for heart disease, I must say that if a pet has advanced heart disease, a combination approach is often best. I have found that many dogs with heart disease or mild heart failure can be maintained on coenzyme Q10, hawthorn, and omega-3 fatty acids plus a natural low-sodium diet without the need for any conventional medications. This approach saves the owner money and requires less monitoring. That's because this natural regimen rarely causes side effects, unlike heart medications. But, for pets with more advanced cardiac disease, these natural therapies will probably need to be used in conjunction with conventional therapies because they are unlikely to be effective by themselves.

KIDNEY DISEASE

Kidney disease in dogs results from any damage to the kidneys. If the damage continues, the kidneys can actually fail. The two types of kidney failure are acute kidney failure and chronic kidney failure.

Acute Kidney Failure

Although acute kidney failure can occur in dogs of any age, most affected pets are younger than 10 years old. Many things can cause acute kidney failure, including ACE inhibitors (such as enalapril), bladder stones, cancer, congenital disorders (such as polycystic kidney disease and renal cortical hypoplasia), heart failure, infections, intrinsic kidney diseases, kidney trauma (including kidney stones and direct trauma), low blood pressure, low blood volume, medications (such as the NSAIDs Rimadyl and EtoGesic), toxins (including antifreeze and aminoglycoside antibiotics), and urethral stones.

Conventional veterinarians treat acute kidney failure with intravenous fluid therapy or peritoneal dialysis to decrease the blood concentration of uremic poisons, antibiotics if needed for infectious causes, antidotes for poisoning, and surgical removal of any blockages or obstructions that may be causing the kidney failure. Many dogs die despite intensive therapy. Those dogs that do recover are considered cured and usually do not have residual kidney damage.

Chronic Kidney Failure

More common than acute failure is chronic kidney failure. Sadly, most of the time veterinarians just don't know what causes chronic kidney failure. It is one of the major causes of illness and death in older dogs. Most dogs with chronic kidney failure are older than 10 years old. The chances of a dog getting it increase as she ages. In fact, most older dogs have some changes in their kidney enzymes on blood tests or changes in the urinalysis that indicates early kidney disease. When caught early, the proper diet, supplements, and sometimes fluid therapy can delay and may even prevent kidney disease from becoming kidney failure.

Some holistic doctors have noticed that since owners began feeding processed pet foods, more dogs are getting kidney disease. It may be that the calcium, phosphorus, and vitamin D that are added to processed foods damage the kidneys. Most holistic doctors recommend feeding properly balanced homemade diets when possible, and advise their clients to avoid any chemicals, such as flea products, and vaccinations when possible.

Finally, because there can be an infectious component to kidney disease and kidney failure, if your dog is at risk, it's important to keep him from getting common infections, especially dental infections.

There is no cure for the damaged kidneys that occur in pets with chronic disease. Most conventional doctors use supportive therapies such as fluid therapy, antibiotics, medications to decrease vomiting that can result from severe kidney disease, drugs to stimulate red blood cell production if anemia occurs, and diets low in protein and phosphorus. It's possible to transplant kidneys, but dogs do not do well with kidney transplantation; therefore, it's rarely done.

Treating Kidney Disease Naturally

Complementary therapies for kidney disease include fluid therapy, omega-3 fatty acids, and herbs to help reduce inflammation in the damaged kidneys.

Fluid therapy. When a dog has kidney disease, he needs more fluids in his body to decrease the concentration of toxic particles in the blood that are normally removed by the kidneys. When a dog is critically ill with kidney problems, a veterinarian will often give him fluids intravenously. Once the dog is stabilized, though, you can continue this important therapy at home. Your veterinarian may teach you how to give your dog fluids by injecting them under his skin.

Omega-3 fatty acids. These fatty acids, EPA and DHA, which are derived from cold-water fish, have been shown to improve kidney function in dogs with kidney disease and kidney failure. This is because they reduce inflammation and improve blood flow to the kidneys.

Flaxseed oil and other sources of omega-3 fatty acids do not have the same positive effects, although small amounts added to the food to help the skin and coat are not harmful.

I recommend giving dogs ½ to 1 gram of omega-3 fatty acids for each 100 calories of food they eat each day. This dose requires a lot of liquid or capsules, so it may be hard to give to your dog. Work with your doctor to find the dose that suits your pet's needs best. In general, shoot for at least two to four times the daily label dosage.

Because fish oil has a mild "blood-thinning" effect, do not give it to your dog if she is taking medications such as warfarin or heparin, except on your veterinarian's advice. Fish oil does not seem to cause bleeding problems when it is taken by itself at commonly recommended dosages.

Herbs. Common herbs, such as astragalus, burdock, dandelion leaf, and marshmallow can detoxify the kidneys. Homeopathics and glandular supplements may also be helpful. Talk with your veterinarian about which remedies are best for your dog and at what dosage.

THYROID DISEASE

Thyroid disease occurs in dogs, as it does in people. In dogs, the thyroid gland produces too little thyroid hormone, causing hypothyroidism.

Hypothyroidism is the most common hormonal disease of dogs, occurring most commonly in middle-aged to older dogs. The average age is seven. Some breeds are more prone to it, including Doberman

pinschers, golden retrievers, Great Danes, Irish setters, Labrador retrievers, old English sheepdogs, and Shetland sheepdogs.

Classic symptoms of hypothyroidism include lethargy, weight gain,
hair loss, oily skin, and chronic skin infections. Less commonly seen
signs in dogs with thyroid disease include neurological disorders, heart
disorders, gastrointestinal disorders, infertility, and behavioral disorders.
Since hypothyroidism is so common in dogs and can cause so many different symptoms, it should be suspected in any sick dog. That's why I
believe that all sick dogs should be tested for thyroid disease.

The three main causes of hypothyroidism are immune-mediated
thyroiditis, idiopathic follicular atrophy, and thyroid cancer. The
first, immune-mediated thyroiditis, is caused when the dog's body
forms antibodies against its own thyroid gland. Some veterinarians
are concerned that this and other immune-mediated diseases may be
caused by repeated vaccinations. In my mind, this is another reason
to minimize the number of vaccinations your dog gets.

The second cause, idiopathic follicular atrophy, happens when
the thyroid gland follicles are lost and replaced by fat or connective
tissue. We're not sure what actually causes this to happen.

Lastly, thyroid cancer, also called adenocarcinoma, can cause hypothyroidism. Thankfully, this is not common in dogs.

Conventionally, dogs with thyroid conditions are treated with
drugs. These drugs are very safe. They are usually given for the life
of the dog because true thyroid disease can't be cured once the thyroid gland has been destroyed. Your veterinarian should test your
dog's blood twice a year to monitor her thyroid levels and adjust the
dosage if needed.

Treating Thyroid Disease Naturally

Complementary medicine has a few things to offer dogs with thyroid disease, including glandular therapy and dietary changes.

Glandular therapy. This type of therapy uses extracts of animal
tissues to treat health problems that affect glands. Dogs with hyper-

thyroidism can be treated with natural (rather than synthetic) glandular therapy. Discuss this option with your veterinarian, who will prescribe it if indicated and discuss the treatment with you.

Dietary changes. As with any condition, the most healthy natural diet is important to improve the dog's overall health. Dogs with thyroid problems have one important dietary restriction: If your dog has thyroid disease, don't feed her cruciferous vegetables, such as broccoli and cabbage. These foods can lower her thyroid hormones even more if eaten in large amounts.

TUMORS AND CANCER

Tumors are very common in dogs, and their incidence increases as dogs age. Sadly, though, younger dogs have been getting cancer more often over the last few years. While cancers can involve the blood, such as lymphoma, or internal organs, such as hemangiosarcoma of the spleen and adenocarcinoma of the liver, many tumors occur on the surface of the dog's body, making it easier for the owner to detect them early.

While most lumps and bumps are benign cysts or fatty tumors called lipomas, some are malignant cancers. I cringe when I hear clients tell me that their former doctors, upon having a tumor pointed out by the clients, say things like "Don't worry. That's just a fatty tumor. We'll wait and watch it and remove it if it gets bigger." How would *you* react if your doctor, upon finding a breast tumor, said "Let's wait and watch and remove it if it causes any problems"?

There is no way I—or any other doctor—can tell if a lump is benign or malignant without testing it first. Simply looking at it, feeling it, and calling it benign is not adequate. In fact, I say it's malpractice! The only exception to this is the obvious appearance of the nonpigmented papilloma (wart), which has a classic appearance and most commonly occurs on smaller, older dogs.

If your dog has any lumps, get them investigated and treated immediately before they cause problems.

On the Case with Dr. Shawn

SASSY

Sassy is a nine-year-old female retriever mixed-breed dog. During her annual physical examination, I pointed out a small lump to her owner. She stated that her previous veterinarian had noticed the lump several months ago, saying that it was probably a "fatty tumor and not to worry about it."

Further questioning of Sassy's owner revealed that the previous doctor did not aspirate or biopsy the tumor, but made his diagnosis just by looking and feeling. I explained to the client that you can't properly diagnose the cause of a tumor by simply looking at the tumor and feeling it. I recommended an inexpensive aspiration cytological examination that I could do right in the office.

She agreed, and I'm glad she did. The microscopic analysis of the tumor aspirate showed a large number of cells filled with purple-staining granules. Sassy had a mast cell tumor.

This type of tumor is cancerous, and sometimes it can spread and be fatal. I removed the mast cell tumor the following day. While it was malignant, it turned out to be a very low-grade malignancy and should not cause Sassy any future problems. The moral of the story is simple: Consider every lump and bump to be cancerous until proven otherwise!

Your veterinarian will most likely do a simple, in-office test called aspiration cytology. This test can quickly be done on most lumps. A tiny needle is painlessly placed into the lump. Cells (or fluid) are easily aspirated from the lump, stained, then examined microscopically. In most cases the doctor can tell if the mass is benign (in which case it may not need to be removed) or malignant (in which case it needs to be removed and biopsied).

Owners ask me occasionally if a surgically removed mass must be biopsied, usually in an attempt to save money. As I was taught by several cancer specialists, if it's worth removing, it's worth biopsying. Only the biopsy can tell us what kind of tumor is present, whether or not the entire tumor was removed, and what additional therapy—such as another surgery, radiation, or chemotherapy—may be needed.

Occasionally, a lump under a dog's skin is too small to test without surgically removing it and having a microscopic biopsy performed. In these cases, these lumps can be safely diagnosed as intradermal cysts. In these cases, I instruct the owner to frequently monitor these lumps and have them tested if they grow. The key here is that most cysts do not grow, whereas both benign and malignant tumors do grow.

Conventional therapies for tumors and cancers include surgery, chemotherapy, and radiation. While most owners fear the side effects that can occur with radiation or chemotherapy in people, most side effects are very rare in dogs.

Treating Cancer Naturally

There are many complementary therapies for cancers and tumors, including DMG; coenzyme Q10; glycoproteins; proanthocyanidins and bioflavonoids; immunostimulant herbs such as alfalfa, aloe vera, astragalus, burdock, dandelion leaf, dandelion root, echinacea, garlic, ginseng, goldenseal, milk thistle, and red clover; immunostimulant mushrooms (maitake, reishi, shiitake); and homeopathic remedies such as *Thuja*, *Viscum album*, and *Arsenicum album*.

Because cancer is such a serious disease, you should think of these therapies as a complement to conventional therapies and not as a replacement for them. I get the best response when I diagnose a cancer or malignant tumor early and combine both conventional and complementary therapies. Discuss your treatment options with your holistic veterinarian and work together to create the best treatment program for your dog.

If for some reason an owner elects not to use conventional therapy, then our only option is to use a complementary therapy. In rare instances, such as advanced liver cancer, no conventional thera-

On the Case with Dr. Shawn

SHENSE

In some cases of dogs with cancer, no conventional therapies are available to help the pet. So it was with the very first cancer patient I ever treated. Shense was a 10-year-old female golden retriever–Chow Chow mix. During her routine annual visit, I felt a large mass in her abdomen. I mentioned this to her owner and told her I wanted to schedule Shense for an x-ray of her abdomen the next day. When I reviewed the x-rays, I saw a large mass in the area of her liver. Her blood profile, which is a normal part of our annual exam that I had drawn during her visit the day before, confirmed the x-ray findings. It showed extremely elevated liver enzymes. Referral to a local cancer specialist confirmed that Shense had advanced liver cancer.

Keep in mind that according to Shense's owners, she never acted sick and seemed "normal." This is not unusual. Dogs often don't act sick until their diseases are quite advanced. Because Shense's entire liver was one big tumor, probably an adenocarcinoma, the cancer specialist had no conventional therapy to offer. Shense was sent home with a very poor prognosis. Most dogs with advanced liver cancer live only a few days to a few weeks after the cancer is diagnosed.

Shense's owner wanted to know if there was anything I could offer to keep Shense alive until Christmas, which was four months away. I

pies are available to treat the dog. In these instances, complementary therapies, such as milk thistle, which can support the liver, are our only hope and may give the dog short-term relief from the cancer. (See "On the Case with Dr. Shawn: Shense" above for an example of this situation.)

Dietary changes. Regardless of what type of cancer is present or what therapy is used, diet is very important to support a dog through her disease. Studies show that dogs with lymphoma lived longer eating a high-protein, high-omega-3 fatty acid diet supplemented with arginine, combined with traditional chemotherapy, compared with dogs on a typical high-carbohydrate diet receiving the same chemotherapy regimen.

was just beginning to learn about using herbs in my practice. I mentioned to her that while I couldn't promise any results, if she was willing to let me prescribe an herbal and nutritional regimen, at least we could try something for Shense. She agreed to do anything, knowing that whatever I prescribed would not hurt her dog and might give her a few more weeks or months of life.

I placed Shense on an herbal detoxifying formula that was designed to heal the liver, as well as various nutritional supplements designed to slow down the growth of cancer. Shense began to improve, put on weight, and had increased energy. While Shense's improvement lasted only two months and she had to be euthanized before Christmas, her owner was happy to have had that extra time with her. She was thankful that Shense did feel better until the end of her life.

Shense's response to my complementary therapies encouraged me to learn more, and her response is typical of most of my cancer patients. Of course, some dogs with aggressive cancers do not respond at all to any therapy. On the other hand, many dogs with cancer live longer than Shense, depending on the type of cancer the pet has and how early we diagnose it. As with Shense's case, complementary therapy may be our only hope for some dogs who have a type of cancer that cannot be helped with conventional surgery, radiation, or chemotherapy.

Many dogs with cancer have small appetites. It is imperative that cancer patients eat. Studies show that both people and pets with inadequate nutrition cannot metabolize the drugs used in chemotherapy. This makes the drugs more toxic and less effective.

One commercial diet, Hill's n/d, is available to help dogs with cancer. The diet contains increased protein, fat, omega-3 fatty acids, and arginine, and decreased carbohydrates. While this diet is very rich due to its high fatty acid content, it is useful as part of the complementary approach to helping the cancer patient.

Because this food is so rich, it gives some dogs diarrhea or makes them vomit. If that's the case with your dog, try a homemade diet that approximates the percentage of nutrients in the n/d diet instead.

(Your veterinarian can recommend the right mix of ingredients.) This gives you total control of the diet and avoids the high temperatures and pressures that occur with all processed diets and destroy valuable nutrients.

WRAPPING UP

As we end Week 5 of our 8 Weeks to a Healthy Dog Program, you have learned many complementary therapies that can help if your dog has one of the common diseases discussed in this chapter. I wish *every* dog could be treated without conventional medicines, which are usually more expensive than complementary therapies and often have side effects which can be worse than the disease being treated. But often, an integrative approach using both conventional and complementary therapies is needed and works best. Work with your doctor if your dog is diagnosed with one of the common diseases discussed in this chapter. Our goal in this program is that if your dog has any disease, you and your veterinarian will incorporate natural therapies whenever possible and use conventional therapies wisely and correctly if they are needed.

Now let's move on to a more cheerful subject in Week 6, where I'll teach you how to use exercise to keep your pet fit and trim—and have fun while you're at it!

8

WEEK 6:
Keeping Your Dog Fit and Trim

In Week 6 of our 8 Weeks to a Healthy Dog Program, we're going to focus on the benefits of exercise for your pet. It's important to understand that true "health" concerns more than just the physical aspects of your dog's life. During the 8 Weeks to a Healthy Dog Program, I strive to work with you and your dog to make your pet healthy all 'round, including his mental health. A regular routine and an exercise program will allow your dog to get in shape mentally, increase bonding between you and your pet (which makes for a healthy emotional side or "spirit"), and definitely make for a happier pet.

We may not translate our knowledge into action (shame on us!), but we all know the importance of a regular exercise regimen for ourselves. Exercise promotes a healthy mental state, improves our cardiovascular capacity, allows for easier digestion of food, relieves stress, promotes healthier blood pressure, tones our muscles, increases our bone strength, improves joint mobility, reduces appetite (unless we exercise too much, in which case appetite may increase), and burns off calories, decreasing body fat. By keeping "lean and mean," we reduce our risk of numerous diseases, including heart attacks, diabetes, arthritis, and cancer.

These same advantages of regular exercise also benefit our canine family members. Remember that in the wild, dogs regularly exercise by running, fetching, hunting, and playing. While they do of course rest, they always seem to be on the move. They need to walk, run, swim, and jump in order to hunt for food, avoid predators, play, interact with pack members, teach their young how to survive, and find mates.

While our pets don't need to hunt, avoid dangers, or mate, they still need to be mobile, run around and play, and burn off excess calories. Exercise also allows dogs to relieve "stress" and work off excess energy, which is vitally important to their emotional and mental well-being. When we confine our pet dogs to a kennel or cage, bathroom, or even a backyard, we remove their normal outlet for exercise.

In doing behavior consultations with clients whose dogs are exhibiting problem behaviors, I commonly find that most of these pets have no regular exercise or routine. This is not a normal condition for dogs, who have evolved to be very energetic, not to be couch potatoes. As a result, these sedentary dogs, who receive minimal or no exercise, often relieve their built-up energy in destructive ways.

Some examples of destructive behavior that are often directly related to lack of exercise and a steady routine include excessive barking, chewing (of the carpeting, furniture, and sometimes of the owner or their own body parts), and inappropriate elimination (the dog deposits urine and/or feces indoors). An important part of therapy for these pets is to develop a regular routine for them, and this routine must include exercise in order to allow the poor dogs to release their built-up energy in a constructive rather than destructive fashion.

WHAT ARE MY DOG'S EXERCISE OPTIONS?

Dogs enjoy variety just like we do, and fortunately, there are plenty of different exercises that you can share with your dog. Examples include walking, running or jogging, swimming, and playing fetch with a ball or Frisbee. As an added benefit, I've found that when I prescribe a regular exercise routine for dogs, the owners often benefit as well. The need to exercise the family dog often gives the owner the push he needs to exercise, too. Many of my clients need a good excuse to exercise, and walking or playing with their canine family members fulfills their needs for healthy exercise.

All of these exercises are valuable. In my opinion, the one that's best for you is often best for your pet. Swimming, if it's an option, is especially helpful for obese dogs and arthritic dogs, as it allows joint movement without placing stress directly on the joints. One word of caution, though: While many dogs can swim, none should be left unattended in the family pool. I've had several patients, both puppies and adult dogs, die while swimming unattended. In some instances, the dog was terrified of the water, panicked, and drowned. In other instances, the dogs were good swimmers but became disoriented, couldn't find their way out of the pools, and drowned from exhaustion.

My own dog, Rita, loves to go for walks around our neighborhood. We also occasionally take her on hiking trails whenever we have the urge to go for a really long walk. While she loves this, because she doesn't do it often, it tires her out later in the day, which ensures she'll have a great night's sleep! For indoor exercise, there's a certain furry mouse toy that she really loves to chase. I'll throw it across the room repeatedly, and Rita races after it and brings it back. As you see, exercise and play can be easy and spontaneous and really don't have to depend upon the weather outside. As long as you encourage healthy movement with your pet, she's using those muscles and other body systems to keep in shape and burn off calories, and the play time increases the bond between you and your pet!

DR. SHAWN SAYS

Simply put, all dogs need a good way to release their normal daily load of energy, and regular exercise allows them to do just that.

DR. SHAWN SAYS

Some owners don't walk their dogs because the dogs have never been properly trained to walk on a leash. If you can't control your dog for leash exercise, work with your veterinarian to find a qualified trainer. Remember that the number-one reason for euthanasia of dogs and cats is behavioral problems. A well-trained dog makes a better pet, and he will live a lot longer!

GETTING STARTED

I recommend starting with 10 to 15 minutes of exercise two or three times each week, and then working up to a daily regimen of 30 minutes or so if you wish. Any exercise is better than no exercise! You'll really enjoy the bonding that occurs with your dog as you exercise together. For variety, you can vary the place as well as the type of activity (walking in the park, swimming, throwing the ball, etc.).

Pets, just like us, must obviously be in good physical shape prior to beginning an exercise program, so let's go back to the veterinary visit prescribed in Week 1 to make sure your dog is in tip-top shape. Talk with your veterinarian to make sure your dog can exercise comfortably and safely. It is the rare pet that can't do some sort of active exercise, even if it's only a short walk around the block two or three times a week. Don't rush exercise! It takes time for most pets (and their owners) to work up to a scheduled 15 to 30 minutes of exercise three to seven times a week.

EXERCISE FOR SPECIAL CONDITIONS

There are several special conditions relating to exercise that are worth mentioning. Here are the most common:

Overweight. Overweight dogs benefit greatly from a regular exercise routine coupled with dietary therapy. Moderate exercise will reduce appetite and burn off calories. Too much exercise, while burning off calories, will make your dog hungrier, defeating the pur-

On the Case with Dr. Shawn

MADDIE

Clients often ask me how much to exercise their dogs. I previously would tell them to listen to their pets. A pet's body will tell you how much it can take. However, I no longer encourage owners to listen to their pets' bodies, based on the following true story. Instead, I tell an owner to listen to her pet's body the day *after* exercise, because this is the best guide to knowing how well the dog can tolerate the amount of exercise done the day before.

Several years ago, I had a young woman working for me as a veterinary assistant. She had a middle-age sheltie named Maddie who had mild to moderate hip dysplasia. On her days off, my assistant would take Maddie to the local park and run and play with her for two to three hours. While the sheltie enjoyed this interaction, it was too much for her. For the next 24 to 48 hours after the playing session, this poor dog could barely move and was obviously uncomfortable. Her owner would be very upset at her dog's pain, wondering what she could do for her.

It was obvious that two to three hours of play once or twice each week was way too much exercise for this dysplastic dog. However, Maddie's owner would never listen to me when I told her to cut back on the amount of exercise per session, and instead try several short play sessions each week. As a result, every week for one or two days following her excessive play sessions, the dog was in pain and the owner was upset. She kept telling me that her dog loved playing for two to three hours and wasn't in pain during their playtime together.

As a result of this case, I now tell owners to observe how their dogs act the day following the exercise session rather than the day of the session. We don't want our pets to suffer from the "weekend warrior syndrome" that so many of us feel after playing hard on the weekends and then finding ourselves barely able to move on Monday morning. This type of activity is *not* the regular exercise program that is so essential to proper mental, emotional, and physical health. The only thing that can come out of the weekend warrior syndrome is unnecessary injury, as we overwork muscles and joints that aren't in shape to handle too much acute stress.

Don't do this to your dog! Work with your doctor to find the best, most comfortable type of exercise that you and your dog can enjoy together, and then have fun!

pose of the diet. Many overweight dogs also suffer from osteoarthritis. Weight loss is critical in helping relieve the stress on
their injured joints. If you have an older arthritic dog, it is imperative that you work to slowly decrease your pet's weight in order to
help relieve the pain of arthritis. Your veterinarian can recommend
the right exercise program for your dog.

ASK DR. SHAWN

**Dear Dr. Shawn: "My dog, Ariel, is severely overweight. We have tried
weight-reduction diets. Is there anything else you would suggest?"**

A: Obesity is the most common nutritional disease of dogs and cats
as well as people. Whenever possible, prevention is the key. That's
because weight loss, as you have experienced, can be difficult to
achieve. Here are some suggestions to help you in your quest to help
Ariel lose her extra weight:

First, make sure your pet does not have medical problems such as diabetes or hypothyroidism. (I will often supplement obese pets with a
thyroid supplement, even if their blood tests are normal, because
sometimes the tissue level may be low, so supplementation may still
benefit the dog.)

If the foods you tried did not help, consider a homemade diet made
with fresh ingredients. A homemade diet is likely to be more palat-
able to your pet than processed foods. You'll find my favorite recipe
on page 87.

Feed small, snack-size minimeals rather than one or two big meals.
Every time Ariel digests food, she burns calories, so if you break her
meals into smaller, more frequent portions, she'll burn more calories
from eating the same amount of food. (A trick we humans can use,
too!) Feeding smaller meals also prevents your dog from becoming
hungry and begging for food. If treats are needed, feed small bites of
raw or steamed vegetables such as carrots. (A cup of vegetables contains about 25 calories.)

A regular program of mild exercise for Ariel will ensure healthy mus-
culoskeletal and cardiovascular systems, improve mental well-being,
and burn off calories.

Heart disease. Dogs with heart disease can benefit from mild exercise, as long as the heart disease is controlled (ideally with supplements rather than with medications that may have side effects) and the pet is not suffering from heart failure. Most dogs with heart disease are asymptomatic when first diagnosed, and a regular exercise routine is not harmful to their hearts. In fact, I believe that it's beneficial.

You can also give Ariel supplements to promote weight loss and improve her overall health. Of course, there are no "magic pills" that will ensure weight loss in pets. Still, there are some supplements you can consider that may contribute to weight loss when used as part of a comprehensive plan. Here are some of the ones I often recommend:

- **Carnitine.** This supplement is recommended in people to reduce fat deposits. Research is needed to determine if this recommendation would be of benefit to overweight pets.
- **Herbs.** Cayenne, mustard, ginger, and other herbs increase metabolism in people and may also do the same in pets. Your doctor can prescribe a safe dose of these herbs if he or she feels they might help your pet.
- **Hydroxycitric acid.** This supplement is extracted from the rind of the tamarind citrus fruit of the *Garcinia cambogia* tree. It suppresses hunger in people and helps prevent the body from turning carbohydrates into fat by inhibiting the ATP-citrate lysase enzyme. (Aren't you glad you asked!)
- **Coenzyme Q10.** Coenzyme Q10 transports and breaks down fat into energy. In people, coenzyme Q10 levels were found to be low in approximately 50 percent of obese individuals. Supplementation with coenzyme Q10 resulted in accelerated weight loss in overweight people. It may be of benefit in overweight pets, and at the recommended dosage no side effects have been seen. Consult with your doctor about using coenzyme Q10 to help in a weight-reduction program for your pet.

Work with your holistic doctor to find the best combination of diet, exercise, and supplementation to help Ariel.

Irritable bowel syndrome. Dogs with irritable bowel disease can benefit from regular exercise, which, as in people, can reduce bowel irritability and normalize bowel movements.

Diabetes. Diabetic dogs can burn off calories during mild exercise. Exercise also drives glucose into the cells of the body and may reduce the amount of insulin needed for proper glucose control.

Hyperactivity. If you have a hyperactive dog, exercise is essential to allow your dog to work off some of his steam. Exercise will reduce the need for medication to calm your pet.

Behavior problems. All pets with behavior problems should have a regular daily routine as well as regular exercise. As dogs are creatures of routine, it is essential for these "problem" dogs to have well-defined daily routines to minimize their stress.

WHAT IF EXERCISE ISN'T AN OPTION?

What about the situations when, for some reason, the owner or pet can't exercise as recommended? Some severely overweight arthritic pets have trouble getting up, much less trying to exercise. Sometimes the weather doesn't cooperate for several days, making it impossible to exercise a pet outdoors. In some cases, the pet owner may suffer from an illness or problem that temporarily prevents her from exercising with her dog.

In these cases, there are several techniques that can be incorporated into your daily routine. These techniques will increase the bonding between you and your dog and help maintain normal muscle and joint tone. Massage, passive manipulation, acupressure, and a technique called TTouch can be helpful in these situations. Let's look at them one by one:

Massage. Massage involves manipulating the muscles in order to stimulate blood and nerve flow and work out any areas of painful inflammation (knots or trigger points). Start with light pressure, especially when working with areas of inflamed muscle tissue, to minimize potential pain to your pet. I myself always enjoy a good deep-tissue massage after working out with weights, as I am prone to developing these trigger points and general muscle soreness. Dogs also enjoy the touching done by their owners during massage. Massage can help rejuvenate muscles after exercise, or simply keep the muscles toned if exercise is not possible.

Passive manipulation. Passive manipulation involves gently moving a joint through its normal range of motion. It is great for dogs with arthritis and pets recovering from bone or joint surgery. Because this can be painful, it's important to take it easy with your dog. A little pain is okay as you break down adhesions in the joint, but your dog should not be terribly uncomfortable. Your doctor or a pet physical therapist can show you how to administer passive manipulation to your pet in order to properly work out each of his joints.

Massage. With your dog lying on her side, kneel close behind her and speak to her in a soft, soothing murmur. Stroke her softly a few times, then begin to methodically press and release each major muscle group. Push firmly but not hard! Continue to reassure her with your voice, keeping it soft and low. When you've finished one side, see if she's relaxed enough to gently turn her over and begin on the other side. Once the massage is over, stroke her gently and leave her to get up on her own.

Acupressure. Acupressure is just like acupuncture, but it's done with your fingers instead of needles. Acupressure is most useful for pets with sore joints. Your doctor can demonstrate the technique of applying pressure to the proper acupuncture points surrounding the joint. By applying pressure to these points, you stimulate blood flow and pain relief to the injured area.

TTouch. TTouch was created in 1978 by Linda Tellington-Jones. The technique employs a series of touches using small, circular finger and hand movements on the body. TTouch has been shown to positively stimulate the nervous system, resulting in a feeling of generalized peace, decreased anxiety, and increased pet-owner bonding. Unlike massage, which activates deeper muscle tissue, the TTouch technique only manipulates the skin and stimulates the nervous system.

While TTouch is not exercise per se, the technique is a wonderful relaxation technique that can help your pet overcome anxiety and fear. For example, many frightened dogs who bite people

TTouch. This technique uses tiny circular movements to calm nervous or frightened animals. If you want to try it, put your fingers together as shown and gently rotate them in circles anywhere on your dog's coat.

(they're called "fear biters") and many dogs who are aggressive when owners try to trim their toenails have shown positive response to TTouch exercises. The TTouch approach allows dog owners to learn new nonthreatening methods of handling their pets; the dogs learn to relax and to develop an improved understanding of their owners' expectations.

The best way to learn TTouch is by observing your veterinarian demonstrate this technique. If he is not familiar with TTouch, I recommend any of the books and videotapes by Linda Tellington-Jones so that you can properly learn the technique.

Any or all of these techniques—massage, passive manipulation, acupressure, and TTouch—can be useful for your pet. A combination of techniques will work on your dog's physical *and* emotional well-being. Most owners can easily learn the techniques and spend 10 to 15 minutes once or twice daily using them on their pets.

WRAPPING UP

As we end Week 6 of the 8 Weeks to a Healthy Dog Program, you and your doctor should develop an exercise program that is easy and enjoyable for you and your dog. I simply can't overstate the positive aspects of any type and amount of exercise. Exercise is useful for its physical and emotional benefits, and it increases bonding between pets and owners. Enjoy this step in the 8-Week Program; you and your dog will both greatly benefit.

Now let's turn our attention to Week 7, where I'll discuss complementary therapies to reduce the need your pet may have for some of the most commonly overprescribed medications: antibiotics, corticosteroids, and non-steroidal anti-inflammatory medications.

9

WEEK 7:
Saying "No" to Drugs
for Your Dog

In this chapter, I'm going to ask you to swim against the stream. Most veterinarians—and most owners—are content to treat sick dogs with drugs. If your dog is sick and you take him to a conventional veterinarian, the chances are good that you'll leave with a prescription. Conventional veterinarians are trained to treat dogs' illnesses with drugs. It's the most powerful weapon in their arsenal.

However, you may already be opposed to medicating your dog. Your instincts may tell you that, while not immediately harmful or directly fatal, drugs are not the best things for your dog. Most medications cause both short- and long-term side effects. While in some instances these drugs can be lifesaving, all too often doctors rely on repeated doses of drugs to cover the symptoms and "treat" the disease rather than correctly diagnosing and healing the dog.

THE QUICK FIX OF DRUGS

Shocking as it is, it's not uncommon for doctors to prescribe drugs for a dog's entire life. Not all of these veterinarians prescribing meds are bad doctors. Conventional medical training just doesn't offer alternatives when it comes to treating disease. Unfortunately, chronic drug therapy doesn't cure problems; it just covers them up. And while drugs may help treat the disease, this approach totally overlooks what is necessary to heal the dog and keep the disease from coming back.

DR. SHAWN SAYS

I believe in using conventional drugs, but only when they're *really* needed. By listening to what the dog's body is telling me, matching the dosage to the dog's need, and using natural treatments for long-term health, I think I give each dog the best treatment possible for him or her.

Some veterinarians prescribe pills because it's easier than figuring out what's actually wrong with a dog. I admit that it does take the veterinarian and owner more time to find out exactly what's making a dog sick. Some doctors and owners simply don't want to take the time to correctly diagnose the problem or find safer, alternative therapies. It's easier to fill another prescription. But this doesn't help the dog, and in some cases the side effects can shorten the dog's life.

Even when a veterinarian does diagnostic testing and the disease is uncovered, it is still all too easy to commit a pet to lifelong drug therapy instead of investigating other alternative therapies that could be equally effective—*without* the side effects.

Some people focus on the finances and choose drugs because they seem like the cheapest solution. It's usually not too expensive to give your pet a shot or pill. But if you look at the big picture, long-term reliance on medications, including the cost of repeated veterinary visits, is often very expensive. In the long run, it's far more costly than a natural approach, which seeks to minimize treatment and optimize health.

THE BENEFITS OF SHORT-TERM USE OF DRUGS

All of that said, I certainly admit there's a place and time for medications. Despite our goal of minimizing the use of drugs as part of our holistic health-care program, sometimes your dog truly may need them. For example, if your dog has a severe infection, antibiotics are definitely indicated. Similarly, dogs with arthritis can safely take NSAIDs like Rimadyl to get through particularly painful days. If your dog has allergies and is scratching his skin raw, short-term steroids may be the way to go.

Using Drugs Wisely

Our goal is to use medications for the shortest length of time possible for relief of symptoms, while waiting for our natural therapies to kick in. Then we rely on natural therapies for long-term control of the illness and healing of the dog. Once the natural therapies kick in, we can wean our dogs off of the conventional medications. In my practice, I find this integrative approach gives the best results with the least number of side effects.

While this approach works for most dogs with illnesses, there are a few rare exceptions. For example, some dogs with multiple severe medical problems, like cancer and autoimmune diseases like lupus, really do require lifelong treatment with conventional medications. Other dogs simply won't tolerate natural remedies, and so their veterinarians are left with conventional treatments. For example, dogs that won't take supplements orally must be injected with medications. Other dogs won't eat a better, healthier diet, even if their owners slave away at the stove to cook it! Still other dogs won't let themselves be bathed two to three times each week in an attempt to heal their inflamed, infected, and itchy skin.

In these cases, the most humane thing we can do is to treat the dog with whatever drug is needed. I don't want any dog to suffer, even if our only course of therapy might cause side effects or shorten the pet's life. In these situations, it's okay to settle for treating the disease with conventional medicine.

When conventional drugs really are needed, I believe the best approach is to tailor the dosages to fit the dog's needs, rather than simply dose all pets equally with a textbook approach. For example, let's say your dog has allergies and needs steroids for quick relief of inflammation and itching. The conventional, textbook approach would be to give her prednisone or prednisolone at 0.25 to 0.50 milligram per pound of body weight daily for seven days, and then slowly wean her to a lower dose for maintenance. The holistic approach might be to use the same starting dose, but only give it for two to three days, and then give her the lowest dose of steroid needed—and only when she's really itchy. By listening to the dog's body, we treat her as an individual and use medications only when she *actually* needs it, not when the textbook says she needs it.

So with all this in mind, our goal is to resist the many temptations to pop pills in your dog's mouth, remembering that the drugs are there if that's really the best solution. In Week 7 of our 8 Weeks to a Healthy Dog Program, we'll look at some of the natural therapies that you and your veterinarian can safely substitute for conventional medications.

THE BIG THREE MISUSED DRUGS

This week, we'll focus on the three types of drugs that are most commonly overprescribed by conventional veterinarians. I call them "The Big Three." They are antibiotics, corticosteroids (which are commonly called steroids), and non-steroidal anti-inflammatory medications (which are called NSAIDs). First, I'll explain why we sometimes need to use these medications. Then, I'll discuss the most intelligent, conscientious way to use them. Finally, I'll talk about some natural therapies that can reduce your pet's dependency on these medications when possible.

Antibiotics

Heralded as "miracle drugs," antibiotics allow us to fight off harmful and potentially fatal bacteria. Since their introduction more than 50

Common Side Effects of Antibiotics, Corticosteroids, and NSAIDS

Like most conventional medicines, antibiotics, corticosteroids, and non-steroidal anti-inflammatory medications have many side effects. Here are some of the most common:

SIDE EFFECTS OF ANTIBIOTICS

Beware of these side effects of antibiotics:

Allergic reaction
Bacterial resistance
Diarrhea
Dry eyes
Fever
Immune-mediated anemias and platelet problems
Immune-mediated joint inflammation
Vomiting
Yeast infections

SIDE EFFECTS OF CORTICOSTEROIDS

Keep a close eye on your dog for these possible side effects if he is taking corticosteroids:

Abnormal laboratory test results
Addison's disease
Cushing's disease
Diabetes
Hyperactivity
Increased appetite
Increased susceptibility to infections
Increased urination
Increased water intake
Lethargy
Obesity
Osteoporosis
Pancreatitis
Progression of cartilage destruction

SIDE EFFECTS OF NSAIDS

Watch out for these side effects if your dog is taking any NSAIDs:

Gastrointestinal ulceration or perforation
Kidney disease
Liver disease
Progression of cartilage destruction

years ago, fewer dogs have died of infectious diseases such as distemper and parvoviral infections. Now, the most common causes of disease in pets are degenerative, such as cancer, heart disease, and kidney disease.

Therefore, while we still see infectious conditions in dogs, they are not the most commonly diagnosed diseases. As a result, most medical conditions in pets will not require long-term use of antibiotics. And for minor infections, such as minor skin infections that may also respond to natural therapies, it's worth trying these alternative therapies first and saving antibiotics for when they are truly needed.

While antibiotics can and should be used safely when needed, they are often misused—and too often overused. Because of misuse and overuse, some antibiotics no longer work. Just as in people, the bacteria become resistant to the drugs. Bacteria that were once easily killed have developed resistance to various antibiotics. In some cases the bacteria are becoming even more powerful in their ability to injure and kill dogs. For example, many antibiotics in the penicillin group are no longer effective against the staphylococcal bacterium, a germ that can be potentially lethal.

Here's an example of how antibiotics are misused: Veterinarians commonly prescribe repeated antibiotic therapy for skin diseases. While antibiotics do treat bacterial skin infections, such as pyoderma and folliculitis, they are of no use for other conditions, such as ringworm, immune skin diseases, most cases of mange, and uncomplicated skin allergies. So instead of giving antibiotics for all problems affecting a dog's skin, veterinarians must find out what's actually causing the problem. They can use skin scrapings to check for mange, fungal cultures to check for ringworm, blood tests to evaluate for thyroid disorders (a common cause of chronic skin problems), skin biopsies to test for a number of diseases, and food allergy trials to eliminate food allergies. All of these tests should be performed before giving up and reaching for the prescription pad.

(continued on page 174)

On the Case with Dr. Shawn

SAMANTHA

I was the fourth doctor to treat Samantha, a six-year-old spayed female black cocker spaniel. Thankfully I will be the last. The previous three doctors treated her skin problem with antibiotics. Samantha, like many fine ladies of her breed, was diagnosed at a young age with "chronic allergies and skin infections." Her first doctor did no diagnostic testing to reach this diagnosis. Instead, he chose to treat her with massive doses of antibiotics and steroids. This explains why Samantha is 15 pounds overweight!

Samantha's second doctor also chose not to do any testing. He placed her on even more potent antibiotics and steroids and added antihistamines to the mix.

Her owner, after seeing temporary results that always relapsed when she stopped Samantha's medications, went to yet a third doctor, hoping to find a better approach. This doctor did a lot of expensive diagnostic testing. He, too, concluded that Samantha suffered from "chronic allergies and skin infections." This doctor continued with her prior medications and also prescribed a thyroid supplement and a new, expensive premium diet.

Since Samantha's owner did not see any results despite all of these conventional therapies, and because she was tired of "killing Samantha with drugs," she came to my practice. She hoped more natural therapies could help her dog.

Upon entering the examining room, I noticed a foul odor coming from Samantha's skin, ears, and teeth. Samantha had a skin infection, an ear infection, and periodontal disease. Her owner said that she knew about the odor coming from Samantha's mouth, but the other doctors told her not to worry about it. The odor coming from Samantha's ears was an ear infection, a chronic problem that had been treated with various medications without much success. Ear infections can have different causes, but no diagnostic testing had been done on Samantha.

Based upon the clinical signs I saw and smelled, and the chronic use of antibiotics and steroids, I suspected Samantha had a yeast infection of her ears and skin. Swabs that I took from Samantha's ears and skin confirmed my suspicions. I surmised that the yeast infection occurred due to chronic misuse of antibiotics and steroids and because, in all likelihood, Samantha was an allergic dog. Dogs with allergies are prone to bacterial and yeast infections.

Because Samantha's problem was chronic and severe, I knew I would have to treat her with conventional medications in the short term, plus natural therapies to help her heal quickly and reduce the amount of time she would need to take these potent medications. I prescribed anti-yeast medication and shampoo therapy to heal her skin. After I cleaned Samantha's ears and teeth thoroughly while she was under anesthesia, I gave her ear drops for her infected ears. It was important to clean Samantha's teeth and clear up her periodontal infection because most itchy dogs chew and lick on themselves. A clean mouth means one less source of infection and odor for her skin!

To strengthen Samantha's immune system, I prescribed a more natural diet, without all of the byproducts and chemicals that were in her previously prescribed "premium diet." As a great bonus to the owner, this new diet was also cheaper! I also prescribed several supplements, including omega-3 fatty acids from fish oil and a green food supplement containing barley grass, wheat grass, and alfalfa. I recommended a homeopathic remedy to control Samantha's seborrheic skin that was occurring as a result of her yeast infection. I also prescribed olive leaf extract for its antibacterial, antifungal, and antioxidant activities.

It took some time, but with the proper diagnosis and treatment, I was able to get Samantha's skin problem under control. Once Samantha's skin cleared up, we were able to focus on her allergies by using the same natural diet, antioxidants, and omega-3 fatty acids plus a regular regimen of shampooing and conditioning to minimize her need for more harmful drugs.

In the near future, I will prescribe a weight-loss regimen as well. Losing weight will extend Samantha's life and control odors associated with infections that hide in her excessive skin folds.

On the Case with Dr. Shawn

JOEIE

Joeie, an eight-month-old spayed female Shetland sheepdog, is my own dog. Joeie had allergic dermatitis. Already in her young life, she had two prior skin infections, which cleared up with antibiotics. When her third infection arose just a few weeks after the successful treatment of her second infection, I decided to try something else. I did not want to subject her body to more expensive antibiotic therapy.

I began a treatment regimen at the first signs of her new infection. I took an aggressive approach. I bathed her frequently with anti-bacterial shampoo and a "leave-on" antibacterial conditioner. I gave her food supplements, a homeopathic therapy, and twice-weekly acupuncture treatments to strengthen her immune system. By choosing this natural approach, I was able to totally avoid the oral antibiotics.

Joeie's skin infection was gone within five days! Normally it takes three or more weeks with antibiotics.

In addition to veterinarians prescribing antibiotics for illnesses that antibiotics don't treat, some veterinarians give them for conditions where they are warranted, but they prescribe the incorrect antibiotic or the incorrect duration of therapy. In these cases, too, the antibiotics are less effective than they should be, the dogs may suffer needlessly, and the bacteria can become resistant to the drugs.

In some very rare cases, such as chronic skin or bladder disease that has not responded to other therapies, it is necessary to put a dog on antibiotics for life. Even then, though, alternative therapies such as acupuncture, homeopathy, herbal supplements, and nutritional therapy may be very helpful in reducing or eliminating the need for antibiotics.

NSAIDs

Non-steroidal anti-inflammatory drugs, including aspirin, ibuprofen, phenylbutazone, Rimadyl, and EtoGesic, are often used in older dogs

DR. SHAWN'S TRICKS OF THE TRADE

Here are my favorite natural substitutes for antibiotics. You apply these soothing natural therapies to your dog's skin:

Aloe vera
Antibacterial shampoos for skin infections
Colloidal silver
Herbal rinses, such as German chamomile and goldenseal
Homeopathic nosodes
Olive leaf extract

You give the following treatments to your dog by mouth. (Always check with your holistic veterinarian first!) They are all antibacterial and immune-boosting herbs:

Alfalfa	Ginseng	Red clover
Astragalus	Gotu kola	Sage
Boswellia	Hawthorn	St. John's wort
Burdock	Horsetail	Turmeric
Dandelion leaf	Licorice	Uva ursi
and root	Marshmallow	Yarrow
Echinacea	Milk thistle	Yellow dock
Garlic	Nettle	
Ginger	Oregon grape	

with arthritis. While they can be helpful in reducing pain and inflammation, they often destroy the cartilage of the arthritic joint, leading to more problems down the road. Other side effects of NSAIDs include liver disease, kidney disease, and stomach and intestinal ulcers. Fortunately, there's a better way—many natural remedies relieve pain and inflammation, too. But sadly, instead of taking the time to try out natural therapies for arthritis and allowing for the four to eight weeks it can take for them to start working, many veterinarians reach for the prescription pad.

In my practice, I prefer to use a more natural approach to pain relief. Complementary therapies, including acupuncture and nutritional supplements, are very useful and have helped save many pets from the side effects of drug therapy. In some cases, they have even saved dogs' lives, because many owners resort to euthanasia for pets that can no longer walk.

But as I said, there's a time and place for drugs. In my practice, I do use NSAIDs on a limited basis. Owners keep a small supply of pills on hand and use them only when their dogs have particularly uncomfortable days. (If your dog has arthritis, you may find that cold, wet days are especially painful for him. This type of weather worsens arthritis in most dogs.) I often try homeopathic remedies, such as arnica or hypericum, for dogs with painful, acute flare-ups of their arthritis before I'll use NSAIDs.

Steroids

These powerful drugs are most often misused to control itching from allergic dermatitis in pets. While these drugs do eliminate inflammation and itching, they have numerous side effects and really

---

Doggie Dosages

Even though lots of holistic veterinarians prescribe herbs for dogs, there aren't many companies that make herbal products specifically for dogs. See "Sources for Natural Foods and Supplements" on page 230 for a few who do. Just follow the dosage information on the label. But, if you can't find the herb that you're looking for in a product designed for dogs, simply buy one for people at a health food store. Use the following guidelines as a starting point to adapt the dosages for your dog:

Capsules: One 500-milligram capsule for each 25 pounds your dog weighs, given two to three times daily.

Powders: ½ to 1 teaspoon of powder for each 25 pounds your dog weighs, given two to three times daily.

Tinctures: 5 to 10 drops for each 10 pounds your dog weighs, given two to three times daily.

Fresh herbs: 4 grams of fresh herbs for each 20 pounds your dog weighs, given two to three times daily.

> ### Special Advice for Golden Retrievers
>
> If you have a retriever, ideally he should never take Rimadyl long-term because of a potential reaction that can result in liver failure. Any retrievers that must take this drug should be carefully monitored for liver problems. If an NSAID is needed for a retriever, I prefer Eto-Gesic. This drug has not been shown to cause the liver problems seen in some retrievers receiving Rimadyl.

should not be used for long-term relief in most dogs. Short-term side effects of steroids include increased appetite, urination, and water intake. Very rarely, depression or excitability can occur. Long-term side effects include Cushing's disease, diabetes, infections, liver disease, obesity, osteoporosis, and suppression of the immune system.

 ——————————————————————————

DR. SHAWN'S TRICKS OF THE TRADE

Here are my natural substitutes for NSAIDs. You give the following treatments to your dog by mouth:

Alfalfa	Ginger	Hyaluronic acid
Boswellia	Glucosamine	Licorice
Cetyl myristoleate	Gotu kola	MSM
Chondroitin	Homeopathic	Perna
Dandelion root	arsenicum	Shark cartilage
Devil's claw	Homeopathic	Turmeric
German	hypericum	White willow bark
chamomile	Horsetail	Yarrow

This natural therapy is applied to a dog's skin:

Capsaicin (cayenne)

You can have a trained professional perform these therapies on your dog:

Acupuncture   Magnetic therapy

The first way these potent medications are misused is when they are repeatedly prescribed in absence of a diagnosis, especially if the condition never improves and continues to worsen. This often happens in dogs with chronic skin disease.

Second, steroids are misused when they are given at high doses for minor conditions that might respond to lower doses. This most commonly occurs when allergic dogs are treated with injectable depot preparations of steroids. These depot steroid shots often last in a dog's body for two months or more, yet each time they are given, the length of time they help a dog is shortened. In other words, while the harmful effects of the steroid shot may last for two months or more, the drugs ease itching and inflammation for only two to three weeks. Then, the problem flares up again.

I prefer to use short-acting steroids, and then only when a dog is

DR. SHAWN'S TRICKS OF THE TRADE

I urge you to talk with your veterinarian about these natural supplement substitutes for steroids:

Alfalfa	Ginkgo	Omega-3 fatty acids,
Antioxidants	Goldenseal	especially fish oil
(bioflavonoids)	Homeopathic	Oregon grape
Burdock root	steroids	Red clover
Dandelion	Licorice root	Yarrow
Garlic	Nettle	Yellow dock

Topical herbal shampoos or rinses include aloe vera, calendula, German chamomile, juniper, lavender, licorice, Oregon grape, peppermint, rose bark, uva ursi, and witch hazel. You can buy herbal rinses from your doctor or some pet stores, but I prefer veterinary-prescribed products because many pet store products are not really of the high quality I insist on in my practice.

Frequent shampooing and conditioning are very helpful for dogs with skin diseases.

ASK DR. SHAWN

Dear Dr. Shawn: "My dog, Sheila, gets a DepoMedrol shot for her allergies every month. We know this will hurt her and possibly shorten her life, yet it is the only thing that helps her allergies. Is there anything else we can do?"

A: You don't tell me what other therapies you have tried, but I'll assume you've tried things like antihistamines and fatty acids without success. Here are a couple of ideas I recommend in my book *The Allergy Solution for Dogs*. First, bathing Sheila several times a week will help a lot. Unless she has a secondary bacterial or yeast infection, I prefer natural soothing products for bathing, such as an aloe vera and colloidal oatmeal shampoo followed by a conditioner.

Frequent bathing is essential for dogs with skin disease. Using gentle shampoos will not dry out the dog's skin, but it will reduce the amount of steroid needed to control itching!

Second, I recommend a natural diet. Homemade is best. Third, minimize the use of vaccines. Giving vaccines, which are foreign proteins, might worsen allergies.

I have a lot of success in my practice using natural therapies for dogs with allergies. If steroids are needed, they can be used safely. However, DepoMedrol is not the way to go. This is a potent steroid that lasts in your dog's body for up to two months, yet it controls itching for only two to three weeks in severely allergic pets. A much safer approach is to use the oral steroids prednisone or prednisolone. You can give your dog these drugs for a few days in a row to stop the itching, then stop until the itching resumes. The nice thing about oral steroids is that they leave the dog's system within 24 hours, helping the body recover from the side effects so often seen with steroids. With this approach, Sheila won't have the shortened life you mentioned as a possible complication from DepoMedrol.

really itchy. I rely instead on natural therapies for long-term maintenance to keep the pet comfortable. I have had a lot of success in treating allergic dogs since adopting this holistic approach. Most of my itchy patients only need low doses of oral steroids a few times each year when their allergies flare up.

WRAPPING UP

Reducing—or ideally eliminating—unnecessary use of toxic drugs is an important part of the 8 Weeks to a Healthy Dog Program. Despite our best efforts, some dogs may never be totally weaned from drug therapy. But you should make every attempt to reduce the dosage to the lowest dose necessary to control symptoms. By reducing dependency on unnecessary drugs, your dog can live a longer, healthier life at a lower cost to you.

As we end Week 7 and head into the homestretch of our 8-Week Program, you've learned some natural alternatives to using conventional medications in your dog. Please work with your holistic veterinarian to find what works best for your dog's unique situation. *Don't* stop giving your dog a medication simply because you like one of the alternatives I've mentioned. Your dog may *need* medication for his condition, maybe even for life. Only your doctor can determine, with your help, the best therapy for your dog's condition.

But if you have a choice of a natural or conventional therapy, I hope you'll feel comfortable giving the natural therapy a try. If one natural therapy does not help your pet, there are often many more you can try. And of course, if no natural therapy gives you the desired result, you can always go back to the conventional medication.

Now let's finish our 8-Week Program by learning something that may come as a surprise to you: how grooming can contribute to your dog's good physical and mental health. If you thought grooming was about little bows and doggie perfume, read on!

10

WEEK 8:
Healthy Grooming

As we finish our 8 Weeks to a Healthy Dog Program, we'll turn our attention to your pet's grooming needs. It may seem odd to discuss grooming your pet in a book about pet health. Yet, paying attention to your dog's coat, skin, ears, and nails is very important to maintaining a healthy pet. Why?

Remember that, just as with people, the skin and hair make up the largest organ of your pet's body. While most owners are more concerned with external disease (parasites and tumors) seen on the skin or hair, internal disease such as liver disease, adrenal gland disease, or thyroid gland disease often shows itself *through* abnormal skin and hair. It is vital to constantly examine and groom your pet to allow for early detection of problems that may occur inside as well as outside your dog's body.

Many of the most common diseases my colleagues and I treat, such as allergies, mange, bacterial and fungal hair follicle infections, and external ear infections (technically called *otitis externa*) are related to skin and ear problems. Regular grooming and cleaning of the skin and ears decreases the chance of problems with these areas of the body.

BATHING AND BRUSHING

While many breeds may not need regular professional grooming and clipping, all dogs need regular bathing and brushing. A regular routine of bathing and brushing removes dead skin and hair

DR. SHAWN'S TRICKS OF THE TRADE

Because regular detergent shampoos may be too harsh for repeated bathing and can predispose your dog's skin to excess
drying and flaking, check with your doctor to find a moisturizing,
soothing shampoo and/or conditioner that is safe for regular use.
I recommend aloe vera and oatmeal shampoos and conditioners
for frequent bathing of allergic dogs, and they work great for regular grooming, too. Also ask your veterinarian to show you how to
properly brush your pet, remove matted hair, and correctly and
safely trim overgrown toenails.

and encourages normalization of the skin and hair growth cycles.

In general, weekly bathing will encourage a healthy coat and
skin, reduce "doggie odors," and teach your dog to accept bathing.
You should brush your dog at least once a week. To prevent mats
from forming, it's a good idea to brush long-haired breeds every day.
If your dog spends a lot of time outdoors, either playing and getting
into all kinds of stuff that smells great to dogs but foul to us, or
hunting and getting lots of burrs, briars, weeds, and so on in his coat,
you'll need to bathe and brush more often than my once-a-week
baseline. And any skunk encounters call for immediate action!

Okay, I've convinced you to bathe your dog, right? But why
bother with grooming? One word: mats. Ungroomed medium-
haired and long-haired dogs can easily develop matted hair. Mats can
be uncomfortable, harbor external parasites, and actually cause destruction of the skin and sores if they become wet. If your dog's constantly scratching matted areas, you can bet the mats are pulling and
he's feeling miserable and may even be bruised from the pull of the
mats when he tries to move. Help him be comfortable and parasite-
free by brushing him often. You can use any type of dog brush or
comb. There are many varieties, and I always encourage my clients
to try several to see which kind they and their dogs like best. It's important that both of you be comfortable with the brush, because the

whole point is to brush often!

If your dog has mats and you want to try to remove them yourself, you can carefully clip them off using blunt-nosed scissors or a grooming shaver with a number 40 blade. However, it's best to have your doctor or groomer demonstrate this to you—you'll need to be really careful to avoid cutting your dog's skin. I've found that most owners aren't comfortable de-matting their dogs, and some dogs will resist efforts to de-mat them (especially if the mats are really painful) and need sedation or even anesthesia to have their mats cut out. If you don't want to remove mats yourself,

If you don't have electric clippers, here's a trick for cutting out mats that will keep you from cutting your dog. First, have someone else hold your dog so your hands are free. Then slide a comb between the mat and your dog's skin. Holding the mat away from the comb with one hand, cut it free with blunt-nosed scissors.

your veterinarian or groomer can do it for you. Or better still, keep brushing your dog regularly so he won't have mats in the first place!

If you're not used to brushing your dog, you may wonder where

 ———————————————————————————

DR. SHAWN'S TRICKS OF THE TRADE

I know that bathing some dogs can be quite challenging, especially if they were not trained to be bathed as puppies. For those of you with difficult-to-bathe dogs, here is a bathing tip that I've found makes the experience a bit easier for many pets. Put your dog in the tub and run the water slowly (a handheld shower head makes this easier). Gently pour the warm water over the dog. Most dogs do better if they don't experience rapidly running water that splashes all over them. Of course, if you have a helper to hold your dog while you gently pour the water over her, that will make things even easier.

to start. Here's what I do: I prefer to brush my dog Rita's body first to get her comfortable. I start along her spine and brush down toward her legs. I tackle the inner legs and abdomen after I've finished the general body brushing. Then I use a comb to comb out the "feathering" on her legs. Finally, I use the same grooming comb to comb out the fur on the outer surfaces of her ears.

Rita is a Cavalier King Charles spaniel, so she has different grooming needs than a shorter-haired breed such as a Labrador retriever. Labs and other short-haired breeds don't have the long, silky fur known as feathering on the backs of their legs, so they can just be brushed out and don't usually need combing.

Paw Care

If you're like most owners, you'll find grooming to be fairly easy, especially if your dog has been trained to accept brushing since puppyhood. But grooming the feet can be a challenge if a dog is not accustomed to having his feet handled. Here are three tips that can make paw grooming easier for you.

1. Get your dog used to having his feet handled by making it part of his daily routine. When he's lying down, give him a loving body rub or patting session. Make sure you pick up each paw once he's relaxed. He may let you touch them for only a second at first, but doing it every time will accustom him to it, and he'll soon accept it as part of your display of affection for him.

2. For breeds with short hair, additional grooming of the feet is not usually necessary. Simply make sure the feet are thoroughly washed and rinsed whenever your dog is bathed.

3. For longer-haired breeds, I recommend regular clipping of the hair on the lower legs and underside of the feet in between the footpads. This lessens the accumulation of dirt and prevents matting. I find it easiest to use grooming clippers with a number

On the Case with Dr. Shawn

ARTIE

Artie is a long-haired male mixed-breed dog. His owners, in an attempt to save money, choose to groom Artie themselves. Sadly, they sometimes forget about his grooming needs.

I saw Artie because he was scratching excessively at a spot on his leg. Close examination showed that this spot was wet from Artie's chewing and that he had a skin infection underneath all of the hair on his back. I also saw something quite disgusting that I don't normally see in dogs: maggots. Yes, maggots. Maggots are larval stages of flies that routinely develop in wet, injured areas of the body following egg-laying by the adult flies. And because Artie had not been groomed in quite some time, his long, wet hair attracted the flies to lay their eggs on his moistened skin.

After sedating Artie, we carefully clipped his hair and began the stomach-wrenching task of cleaning his maggot-infested leg. After 20 minutes, the wound was looking better, and I finished with Artie. I carefully instructed the owners to make sure they kept Artie clipped and dry from then on!

40 blade. Your doctor or groomer can show you how to do this.

With any breed, watch your dog's gait and make sure he isn't limping or favoring a paw. If he's acting like a foot is sore, check for thorns, burrs, splinters, or other objects that might get caught in the pads of the feet. If you've been out with your dog in rough terrain or walking near broken glass or hot asphalt, it's smart to check his paws when you get back anyway, just in case. It's easiest to do this when he's lying down as part of his daily rub.

Nail Trimming

It may not be fun, but it's necessary to trim most dogs' nails. I recommend using Millers Forge clippers, available through veterinarians and pet stores. These are heavy-duty clippers, and I use them successfully

on both smaller breeds of dogs
and larger breeds that have stur-
dier nails. They also come with a
nail guard, which minimizes the
chance of cutting the nail too
short ("quicking the nail"). Cutting a nail too short—into the
quick—causes bleeding and pain.

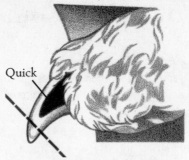

Quick

White nails are easier to clip
because you can see the quick as
a darker area in the center of the
nail. Darker nails are tougher to
deal with, since the quick is not
easily seen. I recommend having
your veterinarian or groomer

Try to locate the quick (the soft,
live center of a nail) before you
cut—if you cut into the quick, it
will hurt your dog and she'll bleed.
Make a slanting cut to shape the
nail. Ask your groomer or veterinarian to demonstrate this technique before you try it yourself!

teach you how to do this before tackling it on your own.

Finally, if you're going to try trimming nails at home, make sure
you purchase some sort of styptic powder, liquid, or stick to minimize bleeding in the unfortunate event that you do accidentally cut
the nail too short.

Clean Ears

Let's not forget our pets' ears, either. Ear disease is common in dogs,
especially if a regular program of ear cleaning is not followed. Certain breeds of dog prone to ear disease (specifically spaniels and retrievers), dogs with chronic ear infections, and dogs that regularly
swim should have their ears cleaned every two or three days. Use a
safe product recommended by your veterinarian. Herbal ear cleaners
containing tea tree oil, peppermint oil, or eucalyptus oil work well.
You can safely remove visible wax with a cotton ball or swab, as long
as you don't reach down into the ear canal any farther than you can
see. Otherwise, you might damage the deeper ear tissues, including
the eardrum.

On the Case with Dr. Shawn

MACK

Mack is a three-year-old neutered male Shih Tzu. He has not had any health problems since I first started treating him as a puppy, except for recurring ear infections. While I do occasionally see ear infections in many different breeds of floppy-eared dogs, most of the breeds with chronic ear disease are retrievers and spaniels. Therefore, I was a bit concerned about why Mack was developing so many ear infections.

I always consider the possibility of allergies in any dog with chronic, recurring skin or ear problems. However, Mack did not have any other signs of allergic skin disease and was never itchy except for his ears. (Though sometimes, chronic ear problems are the only sign seen in allergic dogs.) After discussing bathing and grooming habits with his owner, I figured out Mack's problem. Every time he went to be groomed, the groomer put grooming powder into his ear canals.

Groomers often do this to dry the ears. While the powder does pull moisture away from the ear skin, it also retains that moisture right in the ear canals. Therefore, instead of a dog with wet ears, you have a dog with ears stuffed with wet powder! Bacteria and yeast love to grow in this warm, moist environment. Once my detective work led me to the cause of the problem, solving the problem was easy. I told Mack's owner to tell the groomer not to use any powder in Mack's ears. I dispensed an herbal liquid drying solution that the owner could drop in Mack's ears after bathing and grooming, and I also prescribed a soap-free hypoallergenic shampoo that his owner and the groomer should use on Mack during bathing. This solution solved his problem, and I no longer see Mack for ear infections.

While many groomers get upset when the doctor criticizes a common grooming practice such as placing powder in a dog's ears, owners must take charge and find a groomer to work with them. Veterinarians are trained in skin problems, and it is the wise owner who listens to the doctor and not the groomer when it comes to medical issues such as preventing chronic ear infections. Fortunately, most groomers are more than happy to work with a client to prevent medical problems, and thankfully, most groomers can also detect minor problems like ear and skin infections during the grooming procedure and direct an owner's attention to the need for veterinary intervention.

DOG-FRIENDLY DENTAL CARE

In addition to bathing, conditioning, nail trimming, and ear cleaning, a regular program of dental care (brushing your pet's teeth) will reduce the frequency of periodontal infections. Admittedly, this is difficult for many owners. However, since dental disease is the most common problem in our pets, anything you can do at home to reduce the number of periodontal infections your dog has will be helpful.

Regular dental care will remove plaque from your dog's teeth, so you won't have to take your dog for professional dental cleanings at your doctor's office as often. Ideally, you should brush your dog's teeth daily, but if this is not possible, brush as often as you can. Just as with our teeth, the more you can brush them, the cleaner they will be! Your veterinarian can sell you an appropriate toothbrush and cleaning paste or liquid dental solution and demonstrate the proper technique for brushing your dog's teeth.

ASK DR. SHAWN

Dear Dr. Shawn: "My dachshund, Kelli, has what appears to be dandruff. She is a black-and-tan dog, so it really shows up on her. She is not scratching, and I don't see any fleas on her. Should I be concerned? Is there anything I can do for her?"

A: Dandruff is basically a collection of dead skin cells. It occurs due to an abnormality in keratinization (the normal process of replacing dead skin cells). However, it usually is not harmful or a sign of any specific disease. Having said that, I do recommend seeing your doctor for the problem. There are diseases that can cause excess skin flaking. Various parasites, dietary imbalances, yeast or bacterial infections, allergies, mange, ringworm, and a variety of seborrheas (scaly or oily skin disorders) can cause what appears to be dandruff.

If a visit to your veterinarian does not reveal any of these causes, you can treat dandruff fairly easily. Bathing Kelli with a dog-friendly antiseborrheic shampoo or giving her oral fatty acids (flaxseed oil or fish oil) should be very effective.

DR. SHAWN'S TRICKS OF THE TRADE

Most dogs can be taught to accept toothbrushing if you are patient. I recommend starting with just one tooth to get your dog accustomed to the procedure, slowly working your way through the mouth.

In between brushings, I recommend giving your dog safe chew toys and natural "bones" that can decrease tartar buildup on your pet's teeth. You can give your dog large bones (bones that are too large to fit inside the dog's mouth) safely, and most dogs enjoy them. Chewing these big bones can also help maintain healthy teeth and gums.

Tooth-friendly treats like Greenies (which are edible green bone-shaped treats that contain chlorophyll to decrease breath odor) are also helpful. I don't like to give dogs rawhide treats or pig ears (which are not digestible and may be contaminated with bacteria such as *Salmonella* or *E. coli*) or cow hooves (which are hard and can cause broken teeth).

WRAPPING UP

As we conclude this week, which ends our 8 Weeks to a Healthy Dog Program, you have not only a physically healthy pet but an emotionally healthy pet as well. In eight short weeks, we've done a lot to get your dog on the road to good health.

Keep in mind that while we've spent eight weeks treating diseases and beginning to maximize your dog's health, having a healthy dog is a year-round effort. By feeding a healthy diet, treating diseases as soon as you detect them, and maintaining a regular program of preventive veterinary care, you will greatly improve your dog's health and increase his chance for a long, happy, healthy life.

Health is a choice, just as disease is often a choice. By following the 8 Weeks to a Healthy Dog Program, you have made the choice to have a healthy dog. The program is simple, inexpensive, and also lots of fun for most owners and dogs. Congratulations, and keep up the good work!

I share your desire to maintain health and not simply treat disease. Keep looking for natural solutions to your pet's problems and continue to learn as much as possible. I love to hear from readers, and hope you'll drop me a line and share with me your own success story as you follow the 8 Weeks to a Healthy Dog Program. You can reach me at my e-mail address, naturalvet@juno.com, or write to me (Dr. Shawn Messonier, 2145 West Park, Plano, TX 75075). I extend my best wishes for you and your pet!

Beyond the
8-Week Program

The 8 Weeks to a Healthy Dog Program is a simple, easy-to-follow, and inexpensive program that helps you ensure optimum health for your dog. But what do you do after finishing the program?

The program is not meant to be repeated; rather, it's intended to become a way of life for you and your dog. I hope you will continue to feed the best, most natural diet possible. If illness strikes your pet and a dietary change is required, I hope that you and your holistic veterinarian will work to find the most appropriate food for your dog.

Exercise should be a way of life for you and your dog, and you should continue it throughout his whole life. (As I've noted—and I hope by now you've discovered for yourself—exercise will add so much to *your* life, too!) You can consult with your veterinarian to make adaptations to your dog's routine if illness such as arthritis or injury strikes your pet.

Grooming your dog regularly (brushing, bathing, and clipping if needed) will prevent fur matting and some hair and skin disorders, and it will deepen the bond between you and your dog. You should make it a priority to set aside quality grooming time every week for the rest of your dog's life.

Each year, you should have your veterinarian replace your dog's "annual shots" with a complete physical examination and any necessary laboratory testing (usually some combination of blood tests, a

On the Case with Dr. Shawn

FREDA

Just today, Freda, a 10-year-old female golden retriever, came in with her owner for evaluation of arthritis. According to her owner, Freda was diagnosed with arthritis last year, and she had been prescribed Rimadyl, a popular NSAID medication. During my questioning of the owner and review of the medical records she brought in for her visit, I discovered that Freda had never had x-rays done to properly diagnose the cause of her lameness. The previous doctor just assumed she had hip problems with secondary arthritis and placed Freda on EtoGesic.

Freda's owner also told me that her former doctor had not done regular follow-up visits or blood or urine testing, which are recommended by carprofen's manufacturer. The rest of my visit and examination was unremarkable, except for the discovery of periodontal disease and an evaluation of a small lump on Freda's belly. Freda's owner told me that her former veterinarian had not recommended a dental cleaning despite the periodontal infection because Freda was "too old" for anesthesia. Regarding the small lump on the abdomen, Freda's owner told me that the other doctor had looked at it, felt it, and diagnosed a fatty tumor. No aspirate or biopsy of the mass was done.

During this initial visit, I discussed the 8 Weeks to a Healthy Dog Program with Freda's owner. Since Freda had several problems, we needed to address several aspects of the 8-Week Program during this visit, rather than take the program week by week, as presented in this book. To start with, her owner and I made a list of Freda's problems and prioritized them. (I tell you how to do this in "Week 1: The Veterinary Visit.")

Getting Freda off of her Rimadyl was my goal: I don't like to use this drug with my retriever patients. (It has been linked to a few rare instances of severe liver disease in some retrievers, and long-term use can cause gastrointestinal ulcers and kidney disease.) It may also worsen arthritis, as is typical of members of the NSAID class of medication. Therefore, I

urinalysis, electrocardiogram, and x-rays, similar to the annual testing you receive during your annual physical).

The goal is to diagnose diseases early, *before* your pet becomes ill. I'll say it again: Early diagnosis is less expensive than treating disease.

prescribed a glucosamine supplement, plus an herbal preparation designed to relieve pain and inflammation. (For more on natural treatments for disease, refer to "Week 5: Treating Diseases Naturally.")

I also did blood and urine testing to evaluate all of Freda's organs, but especially her kidneys and liver (as I recommend in Week 1). We discussed Freda's diet (key to her health, as I remind everyone in "Week 3: Choosing the Best Diet for Your Dog"). At this time, we did not change Freda's diet, but decided to wait until the blood and urine tests results were available in case she required a diet for any specific health problems.

I reviewed parasite control (if *you* need a refresher, turn to "Week 2: Treating Parasites") and discussed her vaccination program (as I do with you in Week 1). I suggested that Freda have vaccine titers done in place of immunizations whenever her annual visit was scheduled. Due to her age, I prescribed choline supplementation to help prevent cognitive disorder. (See "Week 4: Choosing Nutritional Supplements for Your Dog" for a thorough discussion of the best pet supplements and when to use them.)

I finally set up a follow-up appointment when we could schedule Freda for x-rays of her hips and spine to confirm the suspected diagnosis of arthritis, clean her teeth, and aspirate and evaluate the lump on her abdomen. I discussed anesthesia with Freda's owner, assuring her that I took a very holistic approach to anesthesia and would plan her anesthetic regimen with her age and health in mind, pending results of our laboratory testing.

I also set up a geriatric plan with Freda's owner, scheduling Freda for reevaluation examinations and laboratory testing every six months. In this way, we could continue the benefits of the 8 Weeks to a Healthy Dog Program for the rest of Freda's life, evaluating each topic in the program during her biannual visits. This approach would allow us the best chance to catch any diseases that might pop up early, *before* Freda became clinically ill.

Early diagnosis also allows treatable diseases to be effectively cured or controlled before serious illness develops and the condition becomes difficult—if not impossible—to treat. For older "geriatric" pets (seven years and older), this examination and laboratory testing

DR. SHAWN SAYS

You are the most important person in your dog's life. *You* decide
what kind of care your pet will receive. Never stop learning and
trying to do the best. Adapt the 8 Weeks to a Healthy Dog Program
to fit your needs and have fun!

should be done twice a year. The incidence of chronic, degenerative
diseases increases as your pet ages, and it's important to detect problems early.

Following the annual visit, most dogs will require a dental
cleaning to make sure that their teeth and gums remain healthy and
their breath remains fresh. (And, as dog owners, we *all* know how
important that is!) As I've mentioned, tooth and gum disease can
lead to serious illness in dogs, so be sure to schedule regular cleaning
appointments with your veterinarian. It's worth it!

Any time your dog becomes ill, or if your veterinarian detects a
problem during the annual visit, you and your veterinarian should
use a natural, drug-free approach to treatment whenever possible.
This is often less expensive than treatment with conventional medications, and side effects are much less common (in fact, they almost
never occur) with a natural approach.

While the 8 Weeks to a Healthy Dog Program officially ends at
the completion of Week 8, the concept behind this natural philosophy never really ends. Go forth armed with the information you've
learned. You'll have the confidence of knowing that you are truly in
control of your pet's health and that you are doing everything possible to keep your dog happy and healthy. Congratulations, and
good luck!

PART THREE

RESOURCES
FOR A
HEALTHY
DOG

APPENDIX 1
Read Before You Feed: How to Read a Pet Food Label

If you choose to feed your dog a processed food, read labels carefully to choose the best from the bunch. Manufacturers must follow specific rules about how to list ingredients, but there are so many technicalities and exceptions that it's difficult to know exactly what's in a food.

The ingredients in pet foods—and the way they affect your dog's health—vary widely. It's important to read the labels to find out if you're buying the best food for your dog's health. But what do those labels mean? Most of the words don't even look like they're in English—they're scientific terms or words used in the food-processing industry that are so specialized they're nearly impossible for a pet owner to understand. To help you decipher the label code, let's take a look at several examples of pet food labels.

I've included four labels to help explain the differences between the various qualities of foods available for your pet. The labels are representative of an inexpensive generic food, a more expensive popular brand of premium food, a natural pet food, and ingredients that might be included in a homemade diet. Following the sample labels, I'll discuss the various ingredients included in each diet. This will help you understand what these ingredients really are and show you how to select a food with ingredients that will enhance your dog's health.

Inexpensive Generic Food Label

Ingredients: Ground Yellow Corn, Corn Gluten Meal, Soybean Meal, Poultry Byproduct Meal, Animal Fat (preserved with BHA), Fish Meal, Meat and Bone Meal, Ground Wheat, Animal Digest, Salt, BHT, Ethylene-diamine Dihydroiodide, Artificial Coloring, Artificial Flavors.

Premium Food Label

Ingredients: Chicken, Brewer's Rice, Ground Wheat, Ground Yellow Corn, Rice Flour, Animal Fat (preserved with mixed tocopherols, a source of vitamin E), Corn Gluten Meal, Egg, Poultry Byproduct, Whey, Vitamin A, D-3, E, B-12, Niacin.

Natural Pet Food Label

Ingredients: Chicken, Brown Rice, Ground Wheat, Ground Yellow Corn, Animal Fat (preserved with mixed tocopherols, a source of vitamin E), Corn Gluten Meal, Egg, Whey, Vitamin A, D-3, E, B-12, Garlic, Rosemary, Rose Hips, Thyme.

Sample Homemade Diet

Ingredients: Chicken, Rice, Vegetables, Olive or Canola Oil, Natural Vitamin-Mineral Supplement.

As you can see, there are several differences in these four labels. Here's how to read them: The first ingredient listed on the label usually represents the number-one ingredient in the food, which is the ingredient contained in the largest amount in the particular food. In the generic food, corn is the most plentiful food contained in the diet. With the premium food, natural food, and homemade diet, an animal source of protein (chicken) is among the first three ingredients listed. In the generic food, an animal source of protein is not listed until the fourth ingredient, and even then it's not actual chicken but poultry byproduct meal.

However, you have to read the labels closely because manufacturers are allowed to "trick" you when listing ingredients. In many instances, the first ingredient may not be the primary foodstuff in the diet due to a technique known as "splitting." Look at that premium label again. Notice that while chicken is the number-one ingredient listed on the label, rice is the number-two ingredient. This would lead you to believe that rice is the second most plentiful ingredient included in the diet. However, ingredient number four is rice flour. Rice flour is defined as "the finely ground meal obtained from milling rice, which contains mostly starch and protein with some fine particles of rice bran." Rice flour is a byproduct and is not as desirable as whole rice. Technically, because "rice" and "rice flour" are different, they can be listed separately. However, they are both rice products, and in this diet, the amount of rice plus the amount of rice flour is greater than chicken. In this premium diet, the number-one ingredient is actually rice.

In this diet, corn is also listed twice, as "ground yellow corn" and "corn gluten meal." Corn gluten meal is "the dried residue of corn protein with the starch and fat removed, and the separation of the bran by a process employed in wet milling manufacture of corn starch and syrup." Corn gluten meal is a byproduct, and it's usually low in health-promoting amino acids, the building blocks of protein. And once again, the combination of corn plus corn gluten meal is greater than the amount of chicken in the diet. By taking time to read the label, the savvy consumer can figure out that splitting has occurred and the diet may not be as great as it first appeared.

To further confuse things, simply by looking at the label it is impossible to tell if the combination of split ingredients is greater than the first listed ingredients. However, knowing that splitting has occurred will tip you off to the fact that the first ingredient listed on the label may not be the primary ingredient in the diet.

WHAT ARE BYPRODUCTS?

Both the generic diet and the premium diet contain "byproducts." What exactly are byproducts? While I used to think that only the cheapest generic foods contained byproducts, I've noticed that many premium brands include one or more byproducts as well. It's impossible to tell exactly what makes up a "byproduct" in each specific diet, as this can vary among manufacturers and even among different diets from the same manufacturer. As a rule, animal byproducts can include any animal parts, such as liver, kidneys, lungs, hooves, hair, skin, mammary glands, connective tissue, or intestinal tract.

While a diet that contains an organ meat such as liver or kidney as its byproduct would be very desirable, a diet containing intestines wouldn't be the best thing for a dog to eat on a regular basis. These less desirable "foodstuffs" don't sound too appealing, and their nutritional value is questionable at best, if not downright harmful. The only way to know what constitutes the byproduct listed on the label is to call the manufacturer and ask.

As the price of the pet food decreases, the reliance of the manu-

Common Byproducts in Dog Foods

It's best to avoid byproducts in your dog's food. Your dog shouldn't be eating those cast-off parts of meats and grains that aren't used in our foods and are relegated to food for our pets. Here's how to spot them on labels:

Meat. If the label says "meat," the food must contain clean flesh from slaughtered animals, such as cattle, sheep, goats, rabbits, and pigs, limited to skeletal muscle or muscle found in the tongue, diaphragm, heart, or esophagus, with or without accompanying fat, sinew, skin, nerve, and blood vessels.

If the label specifies a type of meat, such as chicken, the meat must be from chickens and not other animals.

Meat meal, such as lamb meal. This byproduct is rendered (processed to remove the fat and water) meat without added blood, hair, hoof, horn, hide trimmings, manure, or stomach contents, except in such amounts as may occur unavoidably in good processing practices. It can contain meat from "4D" animals (dead, dying, diseased, or disabled), which comes from animals condemned for human consumption.

Some manufacturers of higher-quality natural dog and cat foods make their own meal, in which case it isn't such a bad thing, so this designation is somewhat vague. As a rule, avoid pet foods containing meat meal unless you contact the manufacturer to find out what exactly is in theirs.

Meat and bone meal. This is similar to meat meal described above, except it can also include bone as well as meat. The amount of meat and bone can vary between batches, so the amount of protein varies as well. Like meat meal, it can contain meat from 4D animals.

facturer on byproducts (especially less desirable byproducts) increases, since byproducts are much less expensive than muscle meats or fish. Using meat or poultry byproducts allows a manufacturer the opportunity to state that his food meets a certain minimum percent concentration of protein. However, the amino acid content (remember, amino acids are the important building blocks of protein) of ingredients like hair, hooves, intestines, and various connective tissues can't possibly meet even the minimum needs of a pet. Yet owners who feed foods with large amounts of byproducts still say that their pets are "healthy!

Meat byproduct. This byproduct is made of nonrendered (so it still contains fat and water), clean animal parts other than meat, including lungs, spleen, kidneys, brain, livers, blood, bone, stomachs, and intestines freed of contents. Meat byproducts cannot contain hair, horns, teeth, or hooves.

While this protein source may be more wholesome than meat meal or meat and bone meal (because it comes from nonrendered tissue and from slaughtered animals rather than from carcasses of already dead animals), there is no way to tell by reading the label how much of which byproducts are included in the food. For example, the byproduct could be liver organ meat (healthy), or it could be intestines (not so healthy). It's best to contact the manufacturer to determine what is contained in their meat byproduct.

Animal byproduct meal. This general term is meant to be for animal byproduct ingredients that don't fit the other categories. It is made of rendered meat without added hair, hoof, horn, hide trimmings, manure and stomach contents, except in such amounts as may occur unavoidably in good processing practices.

Rice gluten meal. This is a byproduct of rice, the dried residue of rice protein without starch or fat. It is low in critical amino acids, so look for a food with ground or whole rice instead.

Corn gluten meal. This is a byproduct of the manufacturing of corn starch and corn syrup. It is the dried residue of corn protein with the starch and fat removed and the bran separated. It is low in critical amino acids, so instead try to find a food with ground corn, which contains the entire corn kernel.

WHICH DIET IS BEST?

In our examples, the diets containing chicken (defined as the "clean combination of flesh and skin, with or without accompanying bone, and does not contain feathers, heads, feet, or guts") as the number-one ingredient would be better choices when looking at the protein ingredients in the food.

But what if a diet that appears to be healthy lists chicken meal as the main ingredient instead of chicken? Would this be acceptable as part of our 8 Weeks to a Healthy Dog Program? Once again, it depends upon what the manufacturer puts in the meal. By definition, a meal contains "the nonrendered clean parts, other than meat, including lungs, spleen, kidneys, brain, livers, blood, bone, stomachs, and intestines freed of contents."

However, some manufacturers have only chicken with water removed as one of the main ingredients. Since the chicken has the water removed from it, it has to be called chicken meal. In this case, the chicken meal contains more "chicken" by weight than the ingredient called "chicken" that contains water plus meat; this would be an acceptable diet. Confusing? Of course, which is why reading a label can only tell us so much. Because some terms such as "meals" can incorporate various types of protein, only calling the manufacturer to find out what is in the meal can tell us anything about the quality of the ingredients used as the protein source.

ARE PRESERVATIVES OKAY?

Finally, notice how each diet is preserved. The homemade diet, being freshly made for the pet, does not require any preservatives. The premium diet and natural diet both use natural preservatives (mixed tocopherols) rather than chemicals to maintain freshness in the food. The generic diet, however, uses the chemicals BHA, BHT, and ethylenediamine dihydroiodide to preserve the food (other chemicals in this diet include artificial colors and flavors). These chemicals, while usually not causing any obvious illness in pets, can cause allergic reactions, irritate the skin and mucus membranes, and affect liver and kidney functions.

While it is probably true that the small amounts of these chemicals put into the food to preserve it won't kill your dog (even if your dog eats this diet his entire life), the goal of our 8 Weeks to a Healthy Dog Program is to minimize the use of chemicals whenever possible. Since many foods are now preserved with natural preservatives, it just doesn't make sense to pick a food with chemical preservatives if other more healthy choices are available.

Of course, as you now know, not everything is as it appears to be when it comes to labeling laws, and even our premium and natural diets may contain chemical preservatives on the labels and not even list them. Look closely at those three processed diet labels again. Notice how they state that the "animal fat" that is added to the diet is preserved with either BHA or mixed tocopherols. It is both possible and permissible that other components of the diet (such as the chicken or chicken meal) are preserved with chemicals, even though it's not listed on the labels.

Here's how this can happen: If the manufacturer of a diet purchases the chicken or chicken meal from someone else, and that someone else adds any preservatives to the meat or meal, the final manufacturer of the diet does not have to list these preservatives on the label because the final manufacturer did not add a preservative to the meat or meal. (In fact, the final manufacturer may not have a clue as to what type of preservative was used by the supplier of the meat or meal.)

Once again, while reading the label can help narrow down good choices of diets from bad choices, in many instances it's still up to you to contact the manufacturer once you narrow down your food choices to find out what type of preservative was used in the meat or meal. It is possible that even some of the "healthy, natural" foods may have some ingredients that have been preserved with chemicals

Common Preservatives in Dog Foods

A major complicating factor when reading labels is that the ingredients are unfamiliar to most people. You certainly wouldn't feed your dog a product that listed "insecticide" on the label, but that's exactly what you're buying if the food contains Ethoxyquin, for example. Read labels carefully to avoid foods with the following chemical preservatives and additives:

BHA (butylated hydroxyanisole). This is a chemical preservative and antioxidant that, while generally regarded as safe in low concentrations, may cause allergic reactions and affect your dog's liver and kidney.

BHT (butylated hydroxytoluene). Although this preservative and antioxidant is believed to be generally safe, it may cause liver and kidney problems.

Ethoxyquin. Depending on the dosage, this preservative, rubber hardener, insecticide, and pesticide may cause cancer.

Ethylenediamine. This solvent, urinary acidifier, and color promoter can irritate the skin and mucus membranes and may cause asthmatic reactions and allergic skin rashes.

Sodium metabisulphite. Another chemical preservative, sodium metabisulphite has caused weakness, loss of consciousness, difficulty swallowing, and brain damage in people.

Sugar, sorbitol, ethylene glycol, and propylene glycol. These preservatives and sweeteners may contribute to diabetes and obesity.

rather than natural preservatives. These diets would not be as wholesome as a homemade diet (made without *any* preservatives), but they would be better than other diets that list chemical preservatives on the labels.

What to choose? In my opinion, if you don't have time to make your dog's meals from scratch, a natural dog food is your best choice. See "Popular Brands of Natural Diets" on page 76 for some foods that I recommend.

APPENDIX 2
Recommended Laboratory Tests

L ab tests offer a critical view *inside* your dog's body to see what's really going on with his health. Here's a schedule of the lab tests that I believe all dogs should receive, along with a physical examination:

All pets, annually. Each year, your veterinarian should do a complete blood count and blood profile, including testing on blood glucose, blood urea nitrogen (to test for kidney function), creatinine (which tests for kidney function), alanine aminotransferase (which measures liver function), total protein, albumin, and an occult heartworm test.

Older dogs, every six months. I believe that dogs seven years of age and older, or five and older for giant breeds, need to see their veterinarians more often: twice a year. This visit should include the tests listed above, plus a thyroid test (usually a Total T4) and urinalysis.

Your veterinarian may choose to do an occult heartworm test every other six-month visit. It needs to be done only once a year.

Dogs with special needs. Dogs with chronic health problems, such as those with kidney disease, should be tested on an as-needed basis, generally every six months. Dogs over 12 years of age, those in whom laboratory values fluctuate, or those whose illnesses are difficult to control should be tested every two to three months.

In addition to the physical exam and the lab tests described above, your veterinarian may choose to give your dog an annual electrocardiogram and x-ray her chest and abdomen, especially if your dog is older.

APPENDIX 3
Recommended Supplements for Healthy Dogs

Every holistic doctor has his own list of personal favorite supplements. I'd like to offer you my recommendations of high-quality products. I'd like you to use this section as a shopping guide. Refer to "Week 4: Choosing Nutritional Supplements for Your Dog" on page 95 for much more detailed information on supplements for your pet.

Let me start with a couple of disclaimers. First, none of the following supplements should harm your dog. They are not drugs, and I've never had a patient become ill taking any of them. Having said that, I do *not* recommend that you use them without veterinary supervision. The main reason for this is to make sure your dog doesn't have an illness that might require a different supplement or therapy. Your holistic doctor must work with you to determine if any of these supplements are right for your pet.

Second, I'm often asked by pet owners if they have to use the supplements sold by their veterinarians. As a rule, the answer is no. However, if you decide to purchase supplements elsewhere, the burden of determining the quality of the supplements is on you. I only recommend supplements from manufacturers I trust, based on my research and experience. Your veterinarian is likely to have carefully considered the products he or she sells as well.

Use the information presented here as a starting point, knowing that I and others have used them with success in our practices.

SUPPLEMENT CHECKLIST

Here are some of the supplements that I recommend for my patients. I'll talk about my favorite brands on page 208.

Puppies

It's great if you're able to start giving your dog supplements while she's still a puppy. Here's what I recommend:

Multivitamin/mineral supplement

Plant enzyme supplement

Also: Consider fatty acids

Consider a green food supplement

Consider a health blend formula

Adult Dogs

Once a dog is out of puppyhood—over a year old—here's what I recommend:

Continue multivitamin/mineral supplement

Continue plant enzyme supplement

Also: Consider fatty acids

Consider a green food supplement

Consider antioxidants when disease arises or as the pet ages

Consider a health blend formula

Geriatric Dogs

Here's what I suggest for dogs seven years of age and older for most breeds, five years of age and older for giant breeds:

Continue multivitamin/mineral supplement

Continue plant enzyme supplement

Continue fatty acids

Continue antioxidants, possibly may need to increase the dosage

Also: Consider a green food supplement

Consider a health blend formula

Consider choline supplement to try to prevent cognitive disorder

Consider coenzyme Q10 to help with many diseases of aging

Consider glucosamine, chondroitin, or hyaluronic acid to try to
  prevent arthritis

Brand Recommendations

To help make your supplement shopping easier, here are some brands that I recommend, from manufacturers that I trust:

Multivitamin/mineral supplements. Nutritional Support, made by Rx Vitamins for Pets, is a wonderful mix of flaxseed, salmon meal, spirulina, bee pollen, kelp, and a number of herbs. Essentials for Dogs is another good supplement from Rx Vitamins for Pets. Canine Plus, which is made by Vetri-Science, is another option.

Enzyme supplements. Once you start looking for them, you'll see that there are several different types of enzymes, including plant enzymes, pancreatic enzymes, and microbial enzymes. I prefer to use plant enzymes because, while all help your dog digest her food better, plant enzymes contain cellulase, which breaks down plant material in the diet. A brand I've had success with is Prozyme.

Fatty acids. Since omega-3 fatty acids found in fish oil have been shown to be helpful in studies, I am partial to these supplements. Other doctors like combination products that contain both omega-3s and some omega-6 fatty acids. Work with your doctor to determine which product might be most successful for your pet's situation.

My favorite product is Ultra EFA by Rx Vitamins for Pets. Its combination of hemp oil and fish oil makes it pleasant-tasting for most pets, and only a small amount is needed when compared with other similar products.

You may also encounter fatty-acid products made from flaxseeds. They're often used as less smelly alternatives to fish oil. The problem is that dogs' bodies can't always use the omega-3s in flax as well as they can use the omega-3s in fish.

Green food supplements. The most common green foods are

barley grass, spirulina, alfalfa, and blue-green algae. They contain lots of nutrients that can prevent and treat illnesses. One brand you could try is Barley Dog.

Antioxidants. My favorite products are NutriPro Antioxidant (made by Rx Vitamins for Pets) and Proanthozone or Proanimal (made by Animal Health Options). These companies make quality products and are committed to the veterinary profession and improving the health of pets. Dr. Robert Silver formulates the products for Rx Vitamins for Pets, and Dr. John Mulnix formulates the products for Animal Health Options. Both are doctors committed to making the best products available. The ingredients in the products are researched and are of human-grade quality. Either supplement can be helpful for a variety of conditions in which oxidative damage is a concern (which means I use one or the other product for just about any disease).

Health blend formulas. I recommend The Missing Link.

Choline supplements. My personal favorite is Cholodin made by MVP Laboratories. I like this so much I actually did the research on the dog and cat products made by MVP. I use this supplement as part of my therapy for cognitive disorder. Not only does choline reverse signs of "doggie Alzheimer's disease," but I believe it can actually prevent the disorder in many dogs. I recommend it for older pets and those with seizure disorders. It is a chewable treat and easily administered to most pets.

Coenzyme Q10 supplements. Talk with your veterinarian about which products he or she prefers.

Joint supplements. There are many joint supplements available. As a rule, the less expensive a supplement is, the less effective it will be. Good joint supplements are not cheap, but they can be cost-effective. Rx Vitamins for Pets, Animal Health Options, and Vetri-Science make some of my favorite supplements. Rx Vitamins makes Nutriflex and Megaflex, Animal Health Options makes ProMotion and Prosamine, Vetri-Science makes the line of Glyco-Flex supplements, and MVP Laboratories makes Cholodin-Flex and CholoGel. I offer my clients a choice, as some pets prefer a chewable pill while others like capsules or powders.

APPENDIX 4
Recommended Herbs for Specific Diseases

Herbal remedies are a powerful tool in the holistic veterinarian's arsenal. Natural and gentle, they treat illnesses with few side effects. In this section, I've listed some common diseases that dogs are plagued by and the herbs that I've found to be most helpful to ease them. (Some herbs have illnesses listed in parentheses behind them. That means that herb is especially good for that condition.)

You can purchase these herbs through your veterinarian or at health food stores. Unless specified, these herbs are to be taken by mouth. If you've been lucky enough to find a product made specifically for dogs, just follow the dosage recommendations on the label. If the product was made for people, refer to "Doggie Dosages" on the opposite page to determine how much to give your dog. Although each condition has several herbs that may help, it's important to try them one at a time and only with your veterinarian's recommendation.

Be sure to check "Side Effects of Selected Herbs" on page 217 and "Herb Interactions" on page 220 before giving your pet any herbal remedies.

Adrenal Gland

Borage (Addison's disease and Cushing's disease)
Licorice (Addison's disease)

Doggie Dosages

Even though lots of holistic veterinarians prescribe herbs for dogs, there aren't many companies that make herbal products specifically for dogs. See "Sources for Natural Foods and Supplements" on page 230 for a few who do. Just follow the dosage information on the label. But, if you can't find the herb that you're looking for in a product designed for dogs, simply buy one for people at a health food store. Use the following guidelines as a starting point to adapt the dosages for your dog:

Capsules: One 500-milligram capsule for each 25 pounds your dog weighs, given two to three times daily.

Powders: ½ to 1 teaspoon of powder for each 25 pounds your dog weighs, given two to three times daily.

Tinctures: 5 to 10 drops for each 10 pounds your dog weighs, given two to three times daily.

Fresh herbs: 4 grams of fresh herbs for each 20 pounds your dog weighs, given two to three times daily.

Allergies

Alfalfa	Ginkgo
Aloe vera	Goldenseal
Burdock root	Licorice root
Dandelion	Nettle
Echinacea	Oregon grape
Feverfew	Red clover
Garlic	Yarrow
German chamomile	Yellow dock

Topically, applying the following herbal rinses to pets with allergies may provide temporary relief: aloe vera, calendula, German chamomile, juniper, lavender, licorice, Oregon grape, peppermint, rose bark, uva ursi, or witch hazel. You can buy herbal rinses from your veterinarian.

Anxiety Disorders

German chamomile   St. John's wort
Kava kava   Skullcap
Passionflower   Valerian

Asthma

Boswellia   German chamomile
Cat's claw   Ginkgo biloba
Coltsfoot   Licorice
Feverfew   Lobelia
Garlic   Turmeric

Bladder Stones and Infections

Alfalfa (to alkalinize urine)   Horsetail
Dandelion leaf   Marshmallow
Echinacea   Oregon grape
Ginkgo (especially for   Plantain
   incontinence)   Uva ursi (to alkalinize urine)
Goldenseal   Yarrow

Cognitive Disorder (doggie Alzheimer's disease)

Alfalfa   Gotu kola
Ginkgo   Horsetail
Ginseng (for its antiaging
   effect)

Constipation

Chickweed   Slippery elm
Dandelion root   Yellow dock
Oregon grape

Diabetes

Bilberry

Burdock root

Calendula

Dandelion leaf

Dandelion root

Garlic

Ginseng

Marshmallow

Yucca

Diarrhea

Aloe vera juice

Boswellia (especially for
ulcerative colitis)

Calendula

German chamomile

Marshmallow

Raspberry leaf

Slippery elm

Epilepsy

Ginkgo

Gotu kola

Kava kava

Skullcap

Valerian

Fleas

Burdock root

Dandelion

Garlic

Red clover

Topically, apply the following herbal rinses:

Canadian fleabane

Feverfew

Mullein

Pyrethrum

Heart Conditions

Bugleweed

Dandelion leaf

Devil's claw (possible
antiarrhythmic)

Heart Conditions—cont.

Garlic

Ginger

Ginkgo

Goldenseal

Gotu kola

Hawthorn

Oregon grape

Immune Stimulation and Cancer

Alfalfa

Aloe vera (try acemannan, a
   derivative of aloe)

Astragalus

Burdock

Dandelion leaf

Dandelion root

Echinacea

Garlic

Ginseng

Goldenseal

Hawthorn

Licorice

Marshmallow

Milk thistle

Nettle

Red clover

St. John's wort

Turmeric

Yellow dock

Infections

Aloe vera

Astragalus

Echinacea

Garlic

Ginger

Gotu kola

Horsetail (especially for
   urinary tract infections)

Licorice

Marshmallow

Oregon grape

Sage

St. John's wort

Turmeric

Uva ursi (especially for
   urinary tract infections)

Yarrow

Topically, apply German chamomile or goldenseal.

Intestinal Parasites

Garlic

German chamomile

Goldenseal

Licorice

Oregon grape

Yarrow

Yucca

Kidney Disease

Astragalus

Burdock

Dandelion leaf

Echinacea

Garlic

Ginkgo

Gotu kola

Hawthorn

Marshmallow

Diuretics

Bugleweed

Burdock

Dandelion leaf

Red clover

Liver Disease

Boswellia

Burdock

Chaparral

Dandelion root

Licorice

Milk thistle

Nettle

Oregon grape

Red clover

Turmeric

Yellow dock

Osteoarthritis and Rheumatoid Arthritis

Alfalfa

Boswellia

Cayenne (apply topically)

Dandelion root

Osteoarthritis and Rheumatoid Arthritis—cont.

Devil's claw

Echinacea (especially for
     rheumatoid arthritis)

Feverfew (especially for
     rheumatoid arthritis)

German chamomile

Ginger

Gotu kola

Horsetail

Licorice

Turmeric

White willow bark

Yarrow

Yellow dock (especially for
     rheumatoid arthritis)

Thyroid Gland

While some herbs—astragalus, bugleweed, and lemon balm—are used to treat hyperthyroidism in cats, they should *not* be used to treat hypothyroidism in dogs. No herbs are currently recommended to treat hypothyroidism.

APPENDIX 5
Side Effects of Selected Herbs

Although herbs are generally safe and mild, they can have side effects and should not be taken lightly. Below, I've listed the herbs most commonly used to treat dogs, along with their most common side effects. Talk with your veterinarian before beginning therapy or stopping conventional medical treatments, even for those herbs listed as safe.

Alfalfa: Generally regarded as safe, but the seeds can cause blood disorders due to L-canavanine and should be avoided.

Aloe vera: Aloe vera is best used externally. If used internally, aloe vera possess strong purgative properties that can result in severe diarrhea due to the anthroquinones located in the latex skin. The juice, while bitter, can be used in small doses and is safer. Aloe extracts, such as acemannan, can be used as injectable medicines or externally on wounds.

Astragalus: The medicinal herb *Astragalus membranaceous* is safe; many other species are toxic. It is best used early in the course of a disease to stimulate the immune system. However, because astragalus stimulates the immune system, avoid it if your dog has a hyperimmune disorder, such as diabetes, or a diminished immune system with low white blood cell counts.

Bilberry: This herb is generally regarded as safe.

Black walnut: This herb is usually considered too toxic to use without veterinary supervision. The tannins and alkaloids may lead to vomiting and diarrhea. Most conventional dewormers (and other herbal deworming preparations) are much safer.

Borage: The leaves of borage contain small amounts of alkaloid compounds that can be toxic to the liver; therefore, don't give it to dogs with liver disease or those that are pregnant. Don't use large amounts of borage or use it for a long time.

Boswellia: This herb can cause diarrhea, skin inflammation, and nausea in people, and possibly in dogs. Don't use it with NSAIDs or give it to dogs that are pregnant or dogs with severe liver or kidney disease.

Bugleweed: It is considered safe, but bugleweed should not be given to pregnant or nursing dogs because it can constrict blood vessels and may have hormonal properties. Do not give it to dogs with hypothyroidism.

Burdock root: Generally regarded as safe.

Calendula: Generally regarded as safe. Calendula should not be given to pregnant dogs because it may stimulate abortion. Calendula contains small amounts of salicylic acid. While the amount is unlikely to cause problems in most cases, take care with dogs sensitive to salicylates.

Canadian fleabane: Veterinarians have little information available regarding the safety of this herb. It may cause allergic reactions in some dogs.

Cat's claw: Cat's claw appears to be safe for dogs, but European doctors believe that it shouldn't be taken with hormones, insulin, or vaccines. Use it with caution for puppies or dogs that are pregnant, nursing, or have severe liver or kidney disease.

Cayenne: Because this herb can be irritating to mucous membranes, don't use it topically on dogs with sensitive skin. Don't give cayenne orally to dogs with sensitive digestive systems or urinary-system disorders, or to dogs that are pregnant.

Chaparral: Because eating large amounts of chaparral can lead to liver damage, do not give it to dogs with liver disease.

Chickweed: This herb is generally considered safe, but the rare dog may be allergic. To check for allergies, apply a small amount to your dog's skin first to check for inflammation, hives, or other signs of sensitivity. If no reaction occurs, feed a small amount and watch for vomiting, diarrhea, or hives. If no reaction occurs, use it as directed by your veterinarian. Note that large quantities may have a laxative effect

Coltsfoot: The flowers (not the leaves or stems) of coltsfoot contain small quantities of alkaloids that can cause liver damage or cancer if taken in large quantities. Use only as directed and for short periods of time. Do not give it to pregnant dogs or dogs with liver disease.

Comfrey: This herb contains small quantities of alkaloids that can cause liver damage or cancer if taken in large quantities. The roots contain the most and should never be used. While the leaves, which are the most commonly used part of the herb, contain almost negligible amounts of alkaloids, use comfrey only as directed and for short periods of time. Do not give it to pregnant dogs or dogs with liver disease.

Dandelion: This herb is regarded as safe.

Devil's claw: Although devil's claw appears to be safe for long-term use, many veterinarians do not give it to dogs with ulcers. Don't give it to dogs with diabetes or dogs that are pregnant. Don't use it at the same time as aspirin, steroids, or NSAIDs.

Echinacea: This herb stimulates the immune system. Don't give it to your dog if he has a hyper-immune disorder or a diminished immune system with low white blood cell counts. It is best used early in the course of a disease at the first signs of infection to properly and fully stimulate the immune system.

Ephedra: Also called ma huang, ephedra is most commonly prescribed for pets with asthma or respiratory problems. It can cause heart arrhythmias and high blood pressure. Use it with great caution in all cases. It should always be combined with other herbs to allow use of the lowest dose of ephedra possible, and it should be used only under veterinary supervision.

(continued on page 222)

Herb Interactions

If your pet needs herbal remedies, remember that herbs are medicines, and they have drug-like actions. Use caution when combining herbs with traditional medications, or if a dog taking herbs is scheduled for surgery. Use the following guidelines if your pet is taking herbal supplements:

HERBS AND SURGERY

Garlic: Stop giving your dog garlic at least one week before surgery, and don't resume therapy until one week after surgery. Garlic can increase bleeding time.

Ginkgo: This herb can lengthen the time it takes the blood to clot in people (and probably dogs). Stop ginkgo supplements about one week before and until 24 hours after surgery.

Kava kava: Since it has been shown to lengthen barbiturate-induced sleep in animals, kava kava should be discontinued 24 hours prior to anesthesia. It may make the effects of similar central nervous system medications stronger.

Valerian: This herb has also been shown to increase barbiturate-induced sleep in animals; caution is suggested with anesthetics and other similar central nervous system medications. Valerian withdrawal syndrome may occur in people (and possibly pets). Wean your dog off valerian over the course of several weeks prior to surgery.

HERBS AND CONVENTIONAL MEDICATIONS

Aloe vera: When taken by mouth, aloe vera can increase the toxicity of certain heart medications, such as cardiac glycosides and antiarrhythmics.

Astragalus: This herb can hinder the immunosuppression of medications, including azathioprine and methotrexate. It can increase the immune-stimulating effects of acyclovir and interleukin-2.

Bromelain: Bromelain can increase the potency of antibiotics and improve the effectiveness of some chemotherapeutic drugs such as 5-fluorouracil.

Burdock: This herb can lower blood sugar levels. Caution is needed for dogs taking insulin.

Cayenne: Cayenne enhances the absorption of theophylline.

Echinacea: Use this herb no longer than several weeks at a time. It can decrease the effects of immunosuppressing medications.

Ephedra: Also called ma huang, ephedra can increase blood pressure, heart rate, anxiety, and tremors due to its activity on the central nervous system. Caution is especially warranted if given with any other medication that has similar activities, including theophylline, phenylpropanolomine, and selegiline. It reduces the effects of dexamethasone by increasing its removal from the body.

Garlic: Because garlic may lower blood sugar levels, caution is needed for dogs taking insulin. Garlic may lengthen the amount of time it takes the blood to clot and should be used with caution if anticoagulants are prescribed.

Ginkgo: Because it can lengthen the time it takes the blood to clot, ginkgo is not recommended for dogs taking anticoagulant medications, such as aspirin and other NSAIDs, PSGAGS, warfarin, coumadin, and heparin.

Ginseng: This herb can strengthen the effects of corticosteroids such as prednisone, prednisolone, dexamethasone, and trimacinolone.

Goldenseal: This herb can increase or decrease the effects of heart medications, such as cardiac glycosides and antihypertensives.

Hawthorn: Hawthorn may increase or decrease the effects of heart medications, such as cardiac glycosides.

Kava kava: When taken together, kava kava may make the effects of similar central nervous system medications stronger.

Licorice: If used with diuretics or corticosteroids, licorice can increase potassium loss. Because it reduces potassium levels, licorice may increase sensitivity of the heart and increase toxicity of cardiac glycosides. It may also make the effects of corticosteroids stronger.

Marshmallow: Marshmallow may retard the intestinal absorption of drugs when given with medications.

Medicinal mushrooms: Mushrooms like reishi may interfere with blood clotting. Use caution if medicinal mushrooms are used with anticoagulant medications such as warfarin or heparin.

Passionflower: Excessive doses of this herb may cause sedation. If your dog is taking drugs that are monoamine oxidase (MAO) medications, passionflower can make the drugs stronger.

St. John's wort: This herb decreases the metabolism of a number of drugs, including warfarin, digoxin, theophylline, and cyclosporine, weakening their effects. But it may make similar central nervous system medications, such as tricyclic antidepressants, stronger.

Valerian: This herb may strengthen the effects of similar central nervous system medications.

White willow bark: Since white willow bark contains acetylsalicylic acid, it should not be used with aspirin or other non-steroidal anti-inflammatory medications.

Feverfew: Don't give this herb to pregnant dogs; it can cause abortion. The fresh leaves can cause mouth ulcers, so only the dried herb should be used. Feed a test dose first to check for oral irritation and sensitivity.

Garlic: Garlic can cause Heinz body anemia in dogs due to the presence of S-methyl cysteine sulfoxide and N-propyldisulfhide. Do not use it for dogs with anemia. If you give your dog garlic regularly, check your pet's blood every few months for anemia.

German chamomile: Avoid German chamomile in pregnant dogs; it may cause abortion. While it is usually considered a safe herb, the rare pet may be allergic to German chamomile, so apply a small amount to the skin first to check for inflammation, hives, or other signs of sensitivity. If no reaction occurs, feed a small amount and watch for vomiting, diarrhea, or hives. If no reaction occurs, use as directed by your veterinarian.

Ginger: Don't give ginger to pregnant dogs or dogs with diabetes. Don't give it to dogs with blood disorders taking anticoagulant medicines. Ginger can increase body temperature, so don't give it to a dog with a fever. Don't use it for dogs scheduled for surgery.

Ginkgo: Do not give ginkgo to pregnant dogs or dogs with blood clotting disorders.

Ginseng: Don't give ginseng to dogs with high blood pressure, bleeding problems, anxiety, or nervousness.

Goldenseal: Do not give this herb to pregnant dogs or dogs with hypoglycemia. Goldenseal may cause hypertension and should not be given to pets with kidney failure. Long-term use can result in excess bile production and can cause vomiting. Current recommendations are to use for no more than seven days at a time.

Gotu kola: Do not give to pregnant dogs. Excessive doses may cause narcotic-like effects, interfere with hypoglycemic therapies, and increase sensitivity to sun exposure.

Horsetail: If your dog has heart disease, high blood pressure, or bladder stones, don't give him horsetail.

Juniper: Don't give your dog juniper if she has kidney disease or if she is pregnant or nursing. Give juniper to dogs with diabetes or heart disease only with your veterinarian's supervision.

Kava kava: Because kava kava can be toxic to the liver in excess, do not give it to dogs with liver disease. Do not give it to pregnant dogs.

Lavender: Because this herb can be toxic to a dog's liver and kidneys, don't give it internally. Don't apply it topically to a place where your dog can lick it off.

Licorice: If you give your dog licorice for more than two weeks at a time, supplement her diet with potassium and decrease her sodium intake by adding dandelion. Use caution in dogs with heart disease or hypertension. In large amounts, steroid overdosage (Cushing's disease) could theoretically occur. It should not be given to pregnant dogs, and care must be exercised with diabetic dogs.

Lobelia: At high doses, lobelia can cause vomiting. Don't use it if your dog is pregnant or nursing. Don't combine it with drugs that can depress the nervous system.

Marshmallow: Use this herb with caution in hypoglycemic pets.

Medicinal mushrooms: Some mushrooms, such as reishi, may interfere with blood clotting; caution is warranted if medicinal mushrooms are used with anticoagulant medications such as warfarin or heparin.

Milk thistle: Do not give milk thistle to pregnant dogs. Long-term use can depress liver function.

Mullein: This herb is generally regarded as safe for dogs.

Nettle: Dogs with allergies may be sensitive to nettle.

Olive leaf: Very rarely, olive leaf can cause diarrhea.

Oregon grape: Do not give this herb to dogs that are pregnant or have liver disease. Excessive dosages may deplete levels of vitamin B complex.

Passionflower: Do not give passionflower to pregnant dogs.

Pennyroyal: Due to potential severe toxicity and death, pennyroyal oil is not recommended for use in dogs.

Peppermint: Don't use this herb at the same time as homeopathic remedies—it can make them less effective. Don't give your dog undiluted peppermint oil. The herb and tea are safe.

Plantain: Some dogs are allergic to plantain.

Pyrethrum: This herb is generally regarded as safe.

Raspberry: Don't give pregnant dogs raspberry.

Red clover: Red clover contains coumadin and should not be given to dogs with blood clotting disorders. If fed in large amounts, the estrogenic components can be toxic. Do not give it to pregnant dogs. Red clover contains small amounts of salicylic acid, so care should be used with pets taking corticosteroids or non-steroidal medications and in dogs who are sensitive to salicylic acid.

Sage: While generally regarded as safe, sage shouldn't be given to pregnant or nursing dogs. It can cause abortion and limit lactation.

St. John's wort: Some dogs may develop sensitivity to sun exposure while taking St. John's wort.

Skullcap: Although skullcap is generally safe, excessive use can cause liver damage. Do not give it to dogs with liver disease or dogs that are pregnant.

Slippery elm: Slippery elm is safe, although a few dogs are allergic to it.

Tea tree: Small-breed dogs may be sensitive to undiluted tea tree oil. Dilute the oil by mixing it with equal parts vegetable oil. Test a small patch of the mixture on your dog's skin prior to use to gauge sensitivity.

Turmeric: Don't give turmeric to dogs with bile duct obstructions, gallbladder stones, or upset stomachs.

Uva ursi: This herb can cause nausea, diarrhea, or vomiting.

Valerian: While valerian is generally safe when used properly, it has been reported to cause nausea and vomiting in high doses in people. While valerian usually induces rest and peaceful feelings, it can cause stimulation in a very few people and pets. As with other sedating herbs, caution is warranted when other similarly acting medications and anesthetics are used. In people, it is recommended to gradually wean patients off of valerian rather than suddenly stop administration of the herb (to prevent valerian withdrawal syndrome). I have not encountered this problem in dogs, but I would encourage slow withdrawal if the herb is used for more than a few weeks at a time. Do not give it to pregnant dogs.

White willow bark: Don't give this herb at the same time as aspirin, steroids, or NSAIDs. It can irritate the stomach if used long term. Don't give it to dogs with aspirin allergies, bleeding disorders, ulcers, kidney disease, liver diseas, or diabetes.

Witch hazel: Use this herb externally only.

Wormwood: Do not give this herb to dogs with seizures, kidney disease, or liver disease. Don't give it to pregnant dogs. Check with your veterinarian for safer herbs for deworming.

Yarrow: Don't give this herbs to dogs that are pregnant. It may cause allergic reactions. Don't use it for long periods of time.

Yellow dock: Do not give yellow dock to pregnant dogs or dogs with intestinal obstructions or intestinal bleeding. Large amounts can cause cramping and diarrhea.

Yucca: Large doses of yucca (in excess of 15 percent yucca root), or yucca taken for long periods of time, can cause vomiting. Do not use for yucca more than five days at a time.

APPENDIX 6
Recommended Homeopathic Remedies for Specific Diseases

Homeopathy is a type of therapy that stimulates the immune system to treat a wide variety of medical conditions. Homeopathic remedies are very small amounts of substances that are diluted anywhere from ten times to millions of times. Holistic veterinarians use homeopathic remedies, usually as tablets, because they are gentle, free of side effects, and inexpensive. I've listed some common dog ailments and suggested homeopathic treatments below. It's very important that you talk with your veterinarian before trying any of the treatments on your dog.

Adrenal Gland

Corticotrophin (ACTH)   Cortisone (Cushing's disease)

Allergies

Arsenicum album   Sulfur (sulphur)
Rhus tox

Arthritis

Bryonia   Rhus tox
Calcarea fluorica   Ruta

Bladder Stones and Infections

Aconitum

Cantharis

Hydrangea

Lycopodium

Bronchitis

Bryonia

Spongia tosta

Diabetes

Syzygium

Uranium nitrate

Diarrhea

Aloe

Arsenicum album

China

Silicea

Epilepsy

Belladonna

Hyoscyamus

Heart Conditions

Adonis vernalis

Crataegus

Strophanthus

Kidney Disease

Aconitum

Phosphorus

Silicea

Liver Disease

Chelidonium

Lycopodium

APPENDIX 7
Natural Alternatives
to Conventional Medications

Antibiotics and corticosteroids, which are commonly called steroids, are two powerful types of drugs that are often over-prescribed by veterinarians. Here are a few natural alternatives you may want to discuss with your dog's veterinarian.

Herbal Alternatives to Antibiotics

Aloe vera

Astragalus

Boswellia (especially for ulcerative colitis)

Echinacea

Garlic

German chamomile (apply topically)

Ginger

Goldenseal (apply topically)

Gotu kola

Horsetail (especially for urinary tract infections)

Licorice

Marshmallow

Oregon grape

Sage

St. John's wort

Turmeric

Uva ursi (especially for urinary system or alkalinized urine)

Yarrow

Herbal Alternatives to Corticosteroids

Alfalfa

Aloe vera

Burdock root

Dandelion

Echinacea

Feverfew

Garlic

German chamomile

Ginkgo

Goldenseal

Licorice root

Nettle

Oregon grape

Red clover

Yarrow

Yellow dock

Natural Alternatives to Anti-Parasitic Chemicals for Intestinal Parasites

Diatomaceous earth (not the kind for swimming pools!)

Garlic

German chamomile

Goldenseal

Licorice

Oregon grape

Pumpkin seed (ground)

Yarrow

Yucca

Natural Alternatives to Anti-Parasitic Chemicals for External Parasites

Burdock root

Canadian fleabane (apply topically)

Dandelion

Feverfew (apply topically)

Garlic

Homeopathic sulfur (apply topically)

Mullein (apply topically)

Peppermint oil (apply topically)

Pyrethrum (apply topically)

Red clover

General Supplements for Dogs with Itchy Skin or Skin Infections

Antioxidants (bioflavonoids)

Colloidal silver

Homeopathic bacterial nosodes

Homeopathic cortisone

Olive leaf

Omega-3 fatty acids (fish oil)

APPENDIX 8
Sources for Natural Foods and Supplements

There are many nutritional supplements and pet foods available for owners who want to share a holistic lifestyle with their pets. I can't list everything I like, but here are some of my favorites. I recommend them for my patients and use them for my own pets.

FOODS

Nature's Variety is my current favorite food. It's loaded with lots of healthy meats, grains, vegetables, and fruits. Most pets love the dry or canned variety. They also make a frozen raw food that can be fed raw or cooked, depending on your preference (or your dog's). This is great for owners who want to feed a raw diet but don't want to prepare it themselves (especially my vegetarian clients!). They also have a super line of real animal bones that are better chew treats than anything else I've seen.

Other natural foods that would make good second choices for me include (in no particular order): Old Mother Hubbard, Halo Purely for Pets, K9 Gourmet, Natura Pet Products, Canidae Pet Foods, Pet Guard, Innova, Solid Gold, and Wysong.

A company called Dancing Paws makes dog treats using only natural, human-grade ingredients. There are several tasty flavors, and your pet will find his own favorite. My dog begs for her treats every day.

You can find all these foods and treats at quality pet stores and in the pet sections of health food stores.

SUPPLEMENTS

There are many supplements that can improve your pet's health—too many to list here! Most of these companies sell only to veterinarians. Your doctor can contact the following companies to get their current listing of supplements.

Acti-Pet
Park City, UT 84060
(800) 669-8877

Animal Health Options
P.O. Box 148
Golden, CO 80402
(800) 845-8849

Bach Flower Remedies
100 Research Drive
Wilmington, MA 01887
(800) 314-BACH

Coastside
P.O. Box 151
Stonington, ME 04681
(800) 732-8072

Dr. Goodpet
P.O. Box 4547
Inglewood, CA 90309
(800) 222-9932

Espree
P.O. Box 3535
Arlington, TX 76007
(800) 328-1317

MVP Laboratories
5404 Miller Avenue
Ralston, NE 68127
(402) 331-5106

Natural Animal Health
P.O. Box 1177
St. Augustine, FL 32085
(800) 274-7387

Nature's Variety
6200 North 56th
Lincoln, NE 68529
(888) 519-7387

Pet Applause, LLC
P.O. Box 250509
Plano, TX 75025
(972) 759-3470

Rx Vitamins for Pets
200 Myrtle Boulevard
Larchmont, NY 10538
(800) 792-2222

Vetri-Science
20 New England Drive
Essex Junction, VT 05453
(800) 882-9993

APPENDIX 9
Recommended Reading

I urge you to check out these books and magazines to learn more about your dog's health. They're among my favorites!

BOOKS

I routinely recommend these good books on holistic pet health.

Becker, Dr. Marty, with Danelle Morton. *The Healing Power of Pets.* New York, NY: Hyperion, 2002. Actually, this one's about how pets heal *people.* I highly recommend it!

Martin, Ann N. *Food Pets Die For,* second edition. Troutdale, Oregon: New Sage Press, 2003. This book is an exposé of the pet food industry. It was one of my inspirations for the diet section of *8 Weeks to a Healthy Dog.* Read it before you feed your pet his next meal!

Messonnier, Shawn, D.V.M. *Natural Health Bible for Dogs & Cats.* Roseville, CA: Prima Publishing, 2001. This is an award-winning book I wrote a few years ago. It is a comprehensive encyclopedia of diseases and complementary therapies, including herbs, supplements, and miscellaneous treatments. It also has a complete section on feeding and preparing diets at home.

———. *The Allergy Solution for Dogs.* Roseville, CA: Prima Publishing, 2000. I wrote this book to teach dog owners how to deal with allergies, a common problem in dogs.

———. *The Arthritis Solution for Dogs*. Roseville, CA: Prima Publishing, 2000. I wrote this book to teach pet owners an integrative approach to dealing with two of the more common medical problems in dogs. A must-read if your dog has arthritis!

Pitcairn, Richard, D.V.M., Ph.D., and Susan Hubble Pitcairn. *Dr. Pitcairn's Complete Guide to Natural Health for Dogs & Cats*, second edition. Emmaus, PA: Rodale Inc., 1995. This is a good book if you're interested in homeopathy and natural diets for pets. A great resource for me!

MAGAZINES

My favorite holistic publications are generally medical journals. However, the magazine I recommend here is a consumer publication I have written for. I think that you will enjoy it!

Animal Wellness Magazine. The only natural health magazine for animals, this magazine is published in Canada and comes out bimonthly. Call (888) 466-5266, or visit their Web site at www.animalwellnessmagazine.com to subscribe.

Index

Boldface page references indicate illustrations. <u>Underscored</u> references indicate boxed text.

Veterinarian *(cont.)*
  owner's role in health care and,
    35–37
  physical examination and, 31–33
  questions for, <u>36</u>
  role of, <u>5</u>
Vitamins. *See* Multivitamins

W
Walking, 157
Warfarin, 135
Wart, 149
"Weekend warrior session," <u>159</u>
Western approach. *See* Conventional
  approach

Wheat germ oil for internal
    parasites, 69
Whipworms, **62**, <u>67</u>
White willow bark
  drug interactions with, <u>221</u>
  side effects, 225
Witch hazel side effects, 225
Wormwood side effects, <u>61</u>, 225

Y
Yard treatments to remove parasites,
    58–59
Yarrow side effects, 225
Yellow dock side effects, 225
Yucca side effects, 225